Deconstructing Management Maxims, Volume I

Deconstructing Management Maxims, Volume I

A Critical Examination of Conventional Business Wisdom

Kevin Wayne

BEP BUSINESS EXPERT PRESS

Deconstructing Management Maxims, Volume I: A Critical Examination of Conventional Business Wisdom
Copyright © Business Expert Press, LLC, 2017.

First published in 2017 by
Business Expert Press, LLC
222 East 46th Street, New York, NY 10017
www.businessexpertpress.com

ISBN-13: 978-1-63157-647-8 (paperback)
ISBN-13: 978-1-63157-648-5 (e-book)

Business Expert Press Human Resource Management and Organizational Behavior Collection

Collection ISSN: 1946-5637 (print)
Collection ISSN: 1946-5645 (electronic)

Cover and interior design by S4Carlisle Publishing Services
Private Ltd., Chennai, India

First edition: 2017

10 9 8 7 6 5 4 3 2 1

Printed in the United States of America

Dedication

To Alysandria and Leanne

Abstract

A contrarian challenge to the status quo, this book vigorously champions healthy skepticism in management theory and practice. Several common management maxims — often taken for granted as truisms — are examined and debunked with evidence-based arguments. The constant repetition of these flawed tropes perpetuates their mythological status and limits personal and organizational performance. Eleven management maxims are rebuked using empirical data, original scholarship, literature reviews, field observations, and thoughtful opinions from numerous experts. Examined in depth, the flawed maxims in Volume One include: Customer is King; People are Our Most Important Asset; Diversity Improves Performance; Competitive Advantage is Necessary to Compete; and A Business Plan is Required for Entrepreneurial Success. The maxims debunked in Volume Two include: Mission Statement is a Must; Learn a Second Language (other than English); Introverts Cannot Lead Effectively; Worrying is Counterproductive; Failure is Not an Option; and Consensus Decision Making is Optimal.

Far from a business as usual business book, *Deconstructing Management Maxims* has been researched with academic rigor yet written in an approachable style. Unafraid of taking on conventional business wisdom, it contains some controversial yet substantiated positions that will provoke critical thinking and debate. After all, sacred cows and long-believed tenets of management lore do not go away quietly. A clear message from this book is that you don't have to believe everything you read or hear— be it in the classroom or at work! It offers a refreshing break from the constant drumbeat of dronish corporate and academic clichés. This book is best appreciated by readers wanting to think critically about important management phenomena.

Keywords

business plan, competitive advantage, consensus decision making, contrarian, customer satisfaction, diversity, English language, failure, human resources, introvert, leadership, management, mission statement

Contents

Acknowledgments

The spirit of evidentiary criticism conveyed in these pages has been influenced by hundreds of authors and their works. A handful of contemporary books stand out, including Phil Rosenzweig's *Halo Effect and Eight Other Business Delusions that Deceive Managers*; Jeffrey Pfeffer's and Robert Sutton's *Hard Facts, Dangerous Half-truths and Total Nonsense*; Pfeffer's *Leadership BS*; Thomas Sowell's *Economic Facts and Fallacies*; Scott Shane's *Illusions of Entrepreneurship*; and *Freakonomics* by Steven Levitt and Stephen Dubner. Needless to say I highly recommend these authors and books, for each in their own way dares to call out commonly accepted yet flawed thinking.

I have used empirical evidence, original scholarship, findings from other scholars, the occasional anecdote, and thoughtful opinions of numerous experts to help communicate my positions. My charge has been to provide a critical examination of common maxims that are improperly viewed as universal truths. I encourage critical thinking and welcome a spirited dialogue related to the content in these pages. Furthermore, my criticism is mindful of how difficult it is to execute in many management situations.

I am thankful to several people for their candid reviews and critiques of early concepts and draft chapters. These thoughtful colleagues and friends include Len Deneault, David Castle, Ray McArdle, Thomas Grover, Curtis Lintvedt, Karen Spohn, and Bob Vartabedian. All of these readers are busy professionals, yet they took time to help me work through and refine the manuscript. I will always remember their generosity.

I have benefited from the assistance of several colleagues in the Division of Business at Rivier University, including Amir Toosi, Susan Farina, Chari Henry-Wilson, and James Hussey. As a lifelong fan of libraries and their staff, I would be remiss not to mention the assistance I received from these remarkable institutions and the professionals that serve them. I am thankful to the staff at Rivier's Regina Library, especially

Holly Klump for her diligent efforts with interlibrary loans and Alan Witt for his work in acquisitions related to my needs. The staff of the Pollard Memorial Library, the Merrimack Valley Library Consortium, and Harvard University's Widener Library have also been helpful and responsive. It should be noted that any errors in this book—be they with regard to grammar, syntax, data, or attributions—are mine and mine alone. My personal opinions expressed in this book do not necessarily reflect the beliefs of any of the fine people or organizations that have assisted me.

I subjected many of my former students to draft chapters, and I am grateful for the feedback in their reflective essays and in-class discussions. Additionally, since many of my positions in this work have been ruminating for several years, I am grateful to past coworkers and superiors that I have learned from—of which there are far too many to name.

It has been a pleasure working with everyone at Business Expert Press and S4Carlisle. From editing to production, the entire team helped make the final stages of the project a smooth and rewarding experience.

Lastly, there are many ups, downs, and late nights involved in this type of project. I have been fortunate to count on my wife, Leanne, for her support and encouragement throughout this long process. For all that and more, I am most grateful.

CHAPTER 1

Introduction

Deconstructing Management Maxims

It's partly true, too, but it isn't all true. People always think something's all true.

—J.D. Salinger, *The Catcher in the Rye*

Thoughtful people mull over inconsistencies.

—Malcolm Gladwell

Tidy absolutes and truisms have always been problematic for those of us afflicted with healthy skepticism. However, if presented with objective data and other credible evidence, I'll drop my guard and embrace the occasional maxim, aphorism, proverb, carbon-dated factoid, or immutable law of physics or chemistry. For instance, I don't question that under normal conditions the freezing temperature and boiling point of water are, respectively, 0°C and 100°C, or that force equals mass times acceleration ($F = ma$), or the principle of Boyle's Law (the volume of a gas varies inversely with the applied pressure).

But in the less precise realms of management and the behavioral sciences, it is unsettling to hear business people confidently dispense phrase-length wisdom that makes a Twitter post read like a Tolstoy novel. The impetus for this book stems from repeatedly witnessing common business axioms incorrectly presented as truisms. Many of these mendacious sayings have transcended our business lexicon by jumping species from management speak to the mundane language of our larger culture.

We casually drop these literary jewels to emphasize key points, using them as evidence to win closing arguments. It is often evidence with no backbone, such as these maxim-inspired assertions: *It's no wonder your business failed, you didn't have a mission statement!* And, *If you had a business plan, you would have known what to do when the market shifted!* Or, how about, *Treat your customers right and they will be loyal.* These absurd claims are representative of the general beliefs that mission statements are akin to oxygen for organizations, that a business plan is a ticket to entering a competitive market, and customer bliss is all you have to worry about to be successful. However, none of these statements are close to being a universal truth. At the root of these flawed exclamations are seemingly harmless maxims. For example, the guilty maxims for the assertions mentioned above are, respectively: *Mission statements are a must*; *Business plans are required for entrepreneurial success*; and the royally dubious decree of *Customer is king.*

The intent of this book is to debunk several sayings that I believe are the worst offenders when it comes to pretending to be global truths, when in fact they are often wrong even when presented as harmless suppositions. For starters, I refer to these pearls of business pseudo wisdom simply as management maxims, and often more succinctly as maxims. A maxim may be defined as a "general truth, fundamental principle, or rule of conduct . . . a proverbial saying."[1] Even the great Aristotle weighed in on maxims, advocating:

> One great advantage of maxims to a speaker is due to the want of intelligence in his hearers, who love to hear him succeed in expressing as a universal truth the opinions which they hold themselves about particular cases. . . . and people love to hear stated in general terms what they already believe in some particular connexion. . . . There is character in every speech in which the choice is conspicuous; and maxims always produce this effect, because the utterance of them amounts to a general declaration of what should be chosen; so that, if the maxims are sound, they display the speaker as a man of sound character.[2]

Apparently even back in ancient Greece it was commonly thought, "We hear what we want to hear." Similarly, management practitioners become conditioned to the general belief systems and lingo of their particular disciplines. Author Chris Mowles, in *Rethinking Management*, alludes to a form of managerial peer pressure, warning of a "universal and dominant currency of management language one must accumulate to be recognized."[3] Buttressed by the writings of sociologist Pierre Bourdieu, Mowles views leadership theories and trends through the lens of managerial social capital. Mowles acknowledges the difficulty with going against the prevailing winds of management thought, speaking about fashionable leadership practices with:

> As they become ubiquitous so they are harder and harder to oppose. To put forward an alternative understanding of leadership, to worry away at the taken for granted assumptions that are left unexplored in currently accepted formulations, is to risk calling one's own professionalism into question.[4]

Bucking the trend or party line can indeed be an occupational hazard. In *Hard Facts, Dangerous Half-truths & Total Nonsense*, Stanford's Jeffrey Pfeffer and Robert Sutton caution us about the incorrectness of conventional wisdom. They claim practitioners in most fields are "unwilling or unable to observe the world systematically because they are trapped by their beliefs and ideologies. Their observations are contaminated by what they expect to see, or because they aren't logical enough in their thinking."[5]

Indeed, hardly just a recent phenomenon, Aldous Huxley alluded to this occupational conundrum and "intellectual inconsistency of men" by writing:

> Men have to live before they think; and to one who would live efficiently, peace of mind is of vastly greater consequence than logical consistency. If peace of mind can be obtained only by sacrificing logic, then logic goes by the board, not merely unregretted, but unnoticed by its generally quite unconscious sacrificer.[6]

Like popular management trends, maxims are hard to dislodge when they attain mainstream appeal. Given that maxims are notoriously succinct and loose in the evidentiary department, many have a corresponding contra maxim. These paradoxical pairs allow the teller to present whichever side of the parable he or she is partial to depending on the situation. For instance, consider the following dueling maxims: *The bigger the better* versus *Good things come in small packages*; *Birds of a feather flock together* juxtaposed with *Opposites attract*; and *It's better to be safe than sorry* pairs neatly and disharmoniously with *Nothing ventured nothing gained.*[7]

A business leader or investor can easily gravitate to a two-sided maxim. For instance, *The bigger the better* is a bite-sized rationale for extolling the economies of scale, market clout, and synergies sure to be had with a large corporation, say a McDonalds's, Toyota or General Electric. It also helps set the table as simplified justification for merger and acquisition activity. While in contrast, *Good things come in small packages* is equally poignant when applied to the nimbleness of small, entrepreneurial ventures or autonomous new product teams unencumbered by large bureaucracies. It works just as well when playing up the benefits of miniaturization or selling smaller cars or shrunken food portions.

In some ways maxims are the ultimate implement in a spin master's communications toolbox: a versatile, two-way convincing device. A maxim permits you to begin a discourse with an innocuous claim. Debaters can enrich an argument with a strategically placed aphorism as filler in between real data or evidence. Additionally, an apropos maxim can be used to seal the deal, for final buy-in or icing on the *case*, if you will. Why take a chance with an original thought when you can rely on concise epigrams of conventional business wisdom?

The maxims treated in this book are, by and large, not of the dueling variety. The lack of dichotomy found in management maxims contributes to their controversy (at least when rebuked). The one-sided nature of management maxims makes them different from general, nonbusiness aphorisms. My attempts at dulling the absoluteness of these proverbs will likely provoke disagreement with some readers. You may not subscribe to the maxim reorientations presented in these pages. My goal is not to reverse the polarities of these statements by hailing their opposite forms. Instead, my objective is to uncover flaws and expose maxims that are incorrectly presented as absolutes. For example, my fight is not with

Customer is king as an ideal, but with *Customer is king* as a patronizing, given, and necessary mantra for a successful business enterprise.

Some of the maxims you will encounter in this book have degraded to the status of, dare I say it, cliché! Cliché is a harsher, more insidious term, summed up as "a trite phrase or expression . . . a hackneyed theme, characterization, or situation . . . something that has become overly familiar or commonplace."[8] To dramatize the deep, 2,400-year-old roots of this device, we turn again to Aristotle as he expounded on the more pedestrian utility of a maxim with, "Even hackneyed and commonplace maxims are to be used, if they suit one's purpose: just because they are commonplace, everyone seems to agree with them, and therefore they are taken for truth."[9]

A prime example of such a hackneyed phrase is the management maxim we examine in Chapter Two: *Customer is king*, a variation of the cliché *the customer is always right*. Oddly enough, *the customer is always right* has limped along as a passé, outdated joke of sorts that remains nostalgically popular via some bizarre form of disaffected group pride. Many regard it as patronizing and untrue, even when stubbornly referring to it. The muttering of *customer is always right* is often accompanied with requisite eye-rolling by both its perpetrators and listeners alike.

Yet *Customer is king* prevails as a surprisingly believable and overused tenet borne of good intentions yet violated by nearly all of our cellphone and cable television companies, city halls, and departments of motor vehicles. What makes *Customer is king* a management maxim worthy of a chapter in this book is that it is often blatantly untrue. We'll get into specifics as to how and why it is so deceitful in Chapter Two, but suffice it to say there are glaring examples of wildly successful firms that only give lip service to this maxim. Indeed, we'll explore how many organizations feel no obligation to subscribe to this battle cry despite our consumer society's insistence that they must. For instance, your cable television provider is very likely a large, profitable company with little regard for you as a customer. *Customer is prey* is a more accurate maxim in many of these cases.

Before previewing the remaining chapters and their respective maxims, we should answer the following question: Why all the fuss about these seemingly harmless proverbial sayings? Surely we can navigate our way around frivolous elements in our vernacular. We must know when we are bending the meanings of these half-truths and corporate myths to fit our sense of style and argumentative purposes, relying on the safety of generalized figures of speech. Are we justifying being *close enough* in terms of the clichéd language and superficial evidence we employ when arguing a point? The problem is these maxims have become so ingrained in our business communication patterns that we have taken them as absolute, literal truths without questioning them in context. Our very notion of truth silently erodes each time some nebulous piece of folklore masquerades as fact. The status quo selfishly guards the implicit approval of our collective naiveté.

For example, when employees hear *Failure is not an option* over and over again from their boss, from films (e.g., *Apollo 13*), and from National Football League (NFL) coaches on television, we internalize and think of it as an absolute truth, a truism. The danger of internalizing this falsehood about failure is that we may not try hard enough, or try at all. We may not discover our performance limits. We may sheepishly avoid all risks, playing *not to lose* instead of maximizing our potential. Think of the implications on research and development if failure were prohibited. If *Failure is not an option* becomes an involuntary, hard-wired response to challenging work situations, we may just sit back defensively and let events unfold around us. Better to be safe than sorry, I guess. We will cover some specific examples relating to the repercussions and benefits of failure later in Volume Two, or at the very least we'll try!

To their credit, maxims are convenient, simple statements that help us explain our world. Maxims function as guidelines and mental models that serve our harried agendas and time-starved decision-making events. For example, a manager may tell her employees to use *Customer is king* as a rule of thumb, so whenever in doubt just be sure to do whatever it takes to make a customer happy. However, the trade-off of this simplification and so-called efficiency may lead to the misreading of problematic situations. Making every customer happy at all costs is not always prudent or possible. Some demanding customers, based on their value to the organization, are not profitable enough for the organization to *over serve*, or maybe even serve at all.

Reliance on maxims is not just a problem confronted by businesses. We find a propensity for passive acceptance of the short and sweet even in science. Physicist Leonard Mlodinow, author of *The Upright Thinkers: The Human Journey from Living in Trees to Understanding the Cosmos*, warns that even when looking at the scientific process, "The oversimplification of discovery makes science appear far less rich and complex than it really is."[10] Indeed, to Mlodinow's point, we often misconstrue scientific achievement in our attempts to dumb it down, making it more digestible or entertaining. Furthermore, the oversimplification of business practices may be even more disquieting than similar violations committed in the hard sciences. As a social science, management is fraught with measurement and validity issues unlike the more quantifiable metrics found in other scientific disciplines.

Another recent example of maxims running amok comes from Spencer Raskoff, CEO of the online real estate service Zillow. Mr. Raskoff claims, "Most axioms are not supported by data, [such as] you should buy the worst house on the best street—that's a terrible idea."[11] Conversely, the dozen homeowners I queried recently thought this to be a sound, value-oriented real estate mantra.

Many people assume that most top performing companies got that way by treating customers exceptionally well, or that these high achieving firms always scored well on *great places to work* or *most admired companies* lists. However, as Phil Rosenzweig points out in *The Halo Effect and Eight Other Business Delusions that Deceive Managers*, most of us think too simplistically and assume—incorrectly—that there is a simple cause-and-effect relationship.[12] Sure there is often (but not always) a strong correlation between superior financial performance of a company and its grade on customer orientation. However, what came first? Did the perception of a customer focus at the company prevail before or after the firm achieved financial success? Did the company become a great place to work because it so successfully exploited its market monopoly power and now offers onsite day care services for employees? Did the creature comforts, premium insurance benefits, and above average salaries cause Google to become a leader in search and online ad revenue? If we are asking if there are clear, cause-and-effect relationships in these questions, the answer is probably no.

Chapters at a Glance, Volume One

As stated earlier, Chapter Two starts us off with the deconstruction of *Customer is king*. Several firms will be identified for systematically violating this maxim, some for going out of their way to treat customers more like prey than kings. Sadly, many successful organizations remain that way in spite of their woeful customer etiquette. I'll include survey data as well as several baffling examples of customer disservice.

Chapter Three, *People are our most important asset*, centers on the hypocrisy of corporate communication doublespeak that stresses how vital employee effort, health, training, and development are to an organization's success. Many companies have outsourced nearly all facets of their human resources (HR) function, much of which is neither human nor resourceful. Thus, where do employees rank in relation to other business assets? I'll provide some sobering evidence on the status of human capital and the general malaise of HR. Globalization, short-time horizons, the rapid pace of automation, and a lack of employee engagement are just some of the challenges facing this largely disposable asset.

A rather controversial topic is our faux maxim for Chapter Four: *Diversity improves performance*. There is some evidence of diversity's benefits with cross-functional teams, problem solving, and strategic thinking. However, there are enormously successful institutions that lack diversity (e.g., the nursing profession; the National Basketball Association; and Silicon Valley's start-up and venture capital communities). Much of the empirical research done on traditional diversity attributes shows little or no support for diversity's impact on organizational performance. The polarizing nature of this topic makes it imperative that we take a dispassionate look at evidence surrounding this phenomenon. A broader scope of what constitutes diversity, including diversity of perspective, as well as ways to more effectively leverage differences in the workforce are discussed.

Chapter Five deals with the notion (held by many smart people) that a *Competitive advantage is necessary to compete*. I will sift through some semantics to clarify what a competitive advantage is and then review several successful firms with no true competitive advantage. However, these firms work hard with what they have and remain viable over time. In fact, you don't have to look far to find sustainable enterprises with no clear competitive advantage. As for the holy grail of strategy, the *sustainable* competitive advantage, that rare and exotic creature belongs on the endangered species list.

The sacrosanct saying that a *Business plan is necessary for entrepreneurial success* is our maxim du jour in Chapter Six, the final chapter of Volume One. How important is it for a fledging entrepreneur to write a formal business plan? Once thought unassailable by mere mortals, there has been a great deal of research looking into the need, use, and effectiveness of business plans. A brief review of the research literature and select case studies are provided to illuminate the false certitude commanded by the business plan requirement. The list of both the freakishly and modestly successful entrepreneurs sans business plan is a long one indeed.

Preview of Volume Two

The much heralded maxim stating that a *Mission statement is a must* is fodder for the first chapter of Volume Two of *Deconstructing Management Maxims*. Although a common inclusion in management, new venture, and strategy texts, as well as a starting point for management consultants to begin invoicing their clients, I have uncovered evidence showing that a mission statement is not as indispensable as once thought. This research has unveiled a surprising number of blue chip firms that do not subscribe to the mission statement mantra. A review of the literature as well as my own data collection and analysis of the S&P 100 and Fortune 500 are provided. Also, there is a short quiz you can take to test your corporate mission knowledge.

Another controversial topic gets the critical treatment in Chapter Two of the second volume. For years, Americans have been bashed for not knowing their world geography and for speaking only English, especially when compared to Europeans. However, I contend that the cry for English speakers to learn a second language is not nearly the necessity it has been portrayed to be. While I am a committed globalist and believer in the richness of intercultural competency, I also subscribe to the widely held position that English is the lingua franca for international business. This chapter examines the growing trend of companies in non-English speaking countries adopting English as their official business language. Yes, that's right, many home-grown companies in non-native

English-speaking countries require their employees to speak English at work—among themselves!

Next up for critical examination is the common yet mistaken notion that *Introverts cannot lead effectively*. Our culture tends to gravitate toward the boisterous and charismatic. We seem destined to follow those with outward confidence, extraverted leaders with enthusiasm and ceaseless energy. In contrast, I'll provide examples of accomplished leaders that are more sedate and reserved, yet as impressive as their chest thumping counterparts.

The act of worrying has gotten a bad rap over the last several years. The misleading maxim of *Worrying is counterproductive* is an outgrowth of all that research telling us how bad stress is for our health. Marriott Hotels ran an ad campaign recently spouting, "When you're comfortable, you can do anything," highlighting the comfy confines of their hotels. However, I'll provide several examples where sweating the details and staying up late pondering *what if* scenarios can yield tremendous benefits. A strong dose of healthy paranoia can be great for business.

The pop sensation maxim *Failure is not an option* is one that warrants particularly thoughtful criticism. While not a desired result, failure happens. If failure is feared too much or rarely seen in you, your team, or your organization, then you are not pushing hard enough for growth and results. This chapter includes numerous examples extolling the benefits of normalizing failure.

Organizations often praise participatory and democratic management systems. The last maxim for discussion in Volume Two, *Consensus decision making is optimal*, has gained momentum from the movement of progressive team management techniques. However, consensus is often employed by risk-averse managers and teams lacking conviction. This tepid behavior is fostered by organizational cultures that are intolerant of dissidents. There are also instances where individuals with positional, expert, or charismatic power may force group members into reluctant consensus. The facade of a team's unified front often takes precedence over making the best decisions.

Each chapter (excluding this one) ends with a handful of contra maxims intended to reflect more of the truth seen in management practice. These contra maxims are not meant to be epigrammatic taunts aimed at their semantic brethren, but are merely reflective of more evidentiary thinking. Furthermore, the list of flawed management maxims presented in these volumes is by no means complete. In the interest of time and space I left several maxims alone and will tackle them in subsequent editions.

Lastly, I have done my best to give a balanced account of the behaviors and implications surrounding the management maxims discussed in this book. I have endeavored to provide the reader with empirical, scholarly evidence from both sides of the maxims. That being said, I have included a pertinent quotation from Albert Madansky of the University of Chicago, who has written and lectured extensively about the great business books of all time. With the reader in mind, Professor Madansky writes:

> The approach taken by most readers today, though, is to overemphasize resonances at the expense of searching for counterexamples. They read their books much like they read the op-ed pages of the daily newspaper, they either agree or disagree with the writer's propositions and leave it at that.[13]

It is the responsibility of the business book writer and reader to challenge assumptions about the behaviors and attitudes of various business stakeholders. Too often, we just accept a given business practice or maxim as gospel without questioning it. Frankly, I expect very few readers to completely agree with my positions in this book, which is fine with me. I hope you read this book and wrestle with many of the maxims analyzed. Compare the examples I provide with your own experiences. Use the premise of each chapter as a launching point with your colleagues to delve into the finer points and implications of specific maxims. Challenge each other's assumptions and evidence. Think critically and reflect. Question the unquestionable. Perhaps this thinking will enhance your management perspectives, career, or organization in some way.

Notes

1. *Merriam-Webster's Collegiate Dictionary, 11th ed.* (Springfield, MA: Merriam-Webster, Inc., 2003). s.v. "maxim."
2. Aristotle, "Rhetoric Book II, Chapters 20–22," in *The Complete Works of Aristotle*, 2nd ed. Jonathan Barnes, 2223–2224 (Princeton, NJ: Princeton University Press, 1984).

3. Chris Mowles, *Rethinking Management: Radical Insights from the Complexity Sciences* (Surrey, England: Gower, 2011), 106.

4. Ibid.

5. Jeffrey Pfeffer and Robert Sutton, *Hard Facts, Dangerous Half-truths and Total Nonsense* (Boston, MA: Harvard Business School Press, 2006), 14.

6. Aldous Huxley, *Proper Studies* (London, United Kingdom: Chatto & Windus, 1927), 82.

7. Richard Nordquist, "What are Dueling Maxims? Examples of Contradictory Maxims, Proverbs, and Aphorisms," http://grammar.about.com/od/qaaboutrhetoric/f/maximqa.htm (accessed May 13, 2015).

8. Merriam-Webster's Collegiate Dictionary, s.v. "cliché."

9. Aristotle, "Rhetoric Book II, Chapters 20–22", 2222–2223.

10. Leonard Mlodinow, "It Is in Fact, Rocket Science," *The New York Times*, 28 May 2015, A19.

11. Spencer Rascoff, "How Did I Get Here?" *Bloomberg Businessweek* May 25–31, 2015, 76.

12. Phil Rosenzweig, *The Halo Effect and Eight Other Business Delusions that Deceive Managers* (New York, NY: Free Press, 2014).

13. Albert Madansky, "How to Read a Business Book," *University of Chicago Magazine, Feb 2001,* http://magazine.uchicago.edu/0102/features/read.html (accessed May 6, 2015).

CHAPTER 2

Customer is King

No capitalist can refuse a chance to cut those heavy personnel costs by transferring jobs to customers who work for free.
—Craig Lambert, *Shadow Work: The Unpaid, Unseen Jobs That Fill Your Day*

You pay for this, but they give you that.
—Neil Young, "Hey Hey, My My (Into the Black)"

It's close to sacrilege to disrespect the anointed institution that is the customer. After all, the customer represents demand, the engine that pulls the train. Be it traditional consumer markets, business-to-business (B2B) segments, government entities, institutions like colleges and hospitals, internal departments, sophisticated channel resellers, professional services, or the growing consumer-to-consumer market—the needs and wants of downstream customers stimulate every organization to perform. You could say the customer is the point, the reason why organizations do what they do.

However, many customers wallow in captive, monopolistic or oligopolistic markets. A veil of customer loyalty masks the prohibitive realities of high brand-switching costs, geographic barriers, poorly served markets, socioeconomic means, and restrictive purchasing contracts. Choice implies options, yet customers are confronted with limited selections in many markets.

The maxim *Customer is king* is a make-believe ideal often meant to distort the true nature of the relationship between buyer and seller. A disingenuous but effective metaphor, *Customer is king* magically transforms one thing into another. Like most metaphors, it doesn't modestly suggest mere association like its more subtle kin, the simile, which uses *like* or *as* (i.e., treat the customer *like* a king, or *as* a king). *Customer is king* is a bolder affront to the senses; senses that when belonging to an average consumer are no match for a commercial system designed to efficiently transact (for a profit), manipulate (to influence attitudes and behavior), and satisfy (for the allure of future business). Incidentally, the satisfaction outcome is conditional and only pursued when necessary.

The objective of this chapter is to debunk the *Customer is king* maxim. I'll provide evidence gathered from the research literature, surveys, corporate communications, personal experiences, and numerous observations from our consumer culture. Sadly, the customer is very often treated as prey rather than king.

No Way to Treat a Royal

First, note that I use *king* as a gender-neutral term. This is merely a reflection of how the concept of customer is generally referred to in a marketing context. For perspective, I present a battery of questions to help frame the dubiousness of the *Customer is king* maxim, including:

Would a king pay his cable television provider more each year while getting less desired entertainment content? Would a king wait in line overnight outside Best Buy for a new i-something? Would a king consistently waive his legal rights by agreeing to arbitration clauses buried in purchase agreements? Would a king grovel and overtip a maître d' for a good table?

Does a king not demand a refund after a bad movie, concert, haircut, meal, or business book purchase? Would a king need protection from the Better Business Bureau, Federal Trade Commission, or Consumer Financial Protection Bureau? Would a king be pleased with a $500 rebate offer on their *next* Volkswagen (VW) purchase after learning of a fraudulent emissions system in their current VW? And speaking of cars, would a king tolerate the typical car-buying ritual perpetrated at most dealerships?

Would a king be duped by manipulative promotions or predatory lending practices? Certainly not a wise monarch. And would Wells Fargo have set up nearly two million sham accounts—without the customers' knowledge—if the bank truly respected their patrons? Lastly, would a king pay to watch a $20 million ballplayer strike out four times, pay nearly $8 for a warm 12-oz beer, wait 10 minutes to use the bathroom, and sit in an uncomfortable seat at Fenway Park on a rainy night in April? Probably not.

Even if the customer was king, he would be a complicated monarch with serious issues. Customers may be more accurately described as irrational, emotional, impulsive, impatient, shallow, socially needy, status seeking, gullible, bored, and hopelessly aspirational.

Some customers are unreasonable and dishonest. They may refuse to provide personal information to marketers in order to protect or conceal their identities, or give incorrect information for the same reasons.[1] Many consumers act like spoiled royals, believing they occupy the moral high ground relative to merchants and producers. Some rogue customers have taken to anonymous and divisive rants on the Internet. It's as though technology has liberated the oppressed consumer class, granting them a new-found power to voice displeasure—whether it's warranted or not. Complaint forums abide the wronged with opportunities to publically howl and rant. The customer feedback dimension of the web functions more like a digital placebo for relieving customer angst. The web's mythical powers of consumer empowerment are seldom actualized. Unknowingly swallowing the hype, buyers view the Internet as a democratizing equalizer, yet the cyber realm is more masterfully exploited by sophisticated producers and sellers.

While there are bad actors on both sides of commercial transactions, most customers are trustworthy souls seeking fairness in transactions that deliver value. The focus in the next several pages will be an investigation into the lack of respect accorded customers by many of their purveyors.

Success Despite Contempt

There are a variety of naughty lists available to help catalogue the worst offenders of customer maltreatment. One such list comes from the financial news and opinion outlet 24/7 Wall St., which conducts a survey of 1,500 randomly selected respondents in order to compile a Customer Service Hall of *Shame*.[2] The worse a firm's customer service score, the higher it ranks in the Hall. Predictably, cable and satellite television providers, cell phone carriers, and banks are the most adept at failing their customers. In Table 2.1, I include the top 10 worst offenders (measured by frequency of "poor" ratings) along with each firm's market capitalization, return on equity (ROE), and brief commentary.

The list in Table 2.1, and others like it, is heresy to those believing in the absoluteness of the *Customer is king* credo. How can certain firms grow while consistently disappointing customers? The answer lies, in part, with imperfect markets, short corporate time horizons, inflated customer expectations, and the insatiable demands of irrational consumers. It's as though some customers actively seek abusive commercial relationships.

Global consulting firm Bain & Company offers some insight as to why wireline communications firms are perennial underachievers in customer service. The Bain & Co. authors explain that:

> These firms thrived in the past as customer acquisition machines, built to grow through rapid penetration of the digital television, Internet and voice products they introduced during the past decade. Their cultures and capabilities haven't adapted to the new reality of greater choice for consumers, including choice of satellite and over-the-top online video alternatives.
>
> They still reward more for new installations than for growth in the number of profitable subscriptions. They invest more in advertising and marketing than in service technicians or in set-top box capabilities that would delight or at least retain customers. And they don't pursue the rewards of customer loyalty as much as they hunt aggressively for new sales to replace departing customers.[9]

The above annotation explains some bad behavior, but it does not completely demystify the industry's reluctance to undergo fundamental change. Comcast, for example, spends heavily on promotional campaigns trying to convince stakeholders that it is prioritizing customer needs (e.g., scheduling installation appointments). This serves as a smokescreen masking the erosion of the value proposition offered to customers. Comcast's long-term survival appears predicated on the success of future acquisitions (like DreamWorks)—not its disregard for current customers.

Table 2.1 Top 10 Customer Service Hall of Shame rankings[8]

Firms with the most "poor" ratings for customer service	Market capitalization	5-year average ROE %	Comments
1. Comcast	$150.3B	13.5%	With regional monopoly power, the *comcastic* treatment of customers will likely get worse with cord cutting, as the firm seeks to maximize margins with remaining customers. The U.S. Government rejected a merger with Time Warner on antitrust concerns. Perhaps Comcast's desire to create entertainment content (e.g., purchase of DreamWorks) will mercifully distance it from consumers.
2. Direct TV	n.a.	n.a.	Acquired by AT&T in 2014 for $49B in cash and stock ($67B when including assumed debt).[3] This merger does not bode well for consumers.
3. Bank of America	$149.2B	2.8%	Fees, fees, and more fees.
4. Dish Network	$22B	–	Employee dissatisfaction is not helping the firm's customer scores.[4] Firm has considered mergers with T-Mobile and Sprint in the past.
5. AT&T	$221.8B	11.3%	Fined $100 million in 2015 by the Federal Communications Commission for reducing data speeds (a.k.a. throttling) of its unlimited data subscribers. The Federal Trade Commission filed suit against AT&T for the same issue.[5]
6. AOL	n.a.	n.a.	Acquired by Verizon in 2015 for $4.4B.
7. Verizon Communications	$210.8B	40.6%	Treats customers as sheep and uses a third party (Asurion) for many phone warranties seemingly to both deflect and increase customer rage.

(Continued)

Table 2.1 *Top 10 Customer Service Hall of Shame rankings*[8] (*Continued*)

Firms with the most "poor" ratings for customer service	Market capitalization	5-year average ROE %	Comments
8. T-Mobile	$31.6B	−65.7%	Smaller than rivals but without a model to differentiate it from others. Hustles customers with the same phone plan shell game that competitors use. Network reliability is rated poorly.[6]
9. Wells Fargo	$241.2B	13.2%	Wells Fargo had a relatively high "excellent" rating in addition to its sizable "poor" rating. Poor scores may be related to general discontent with the banking industry following the last financial crisis.[7] It appears customers either love them or hate them. Note: This survey was conducted before the bank's infamous sham account scandal exposed in 2016, where 5,300 employees were fired for illicitly setting up accounts unbeknownst to customers.
10. Walmart	$214.4B	22.2%	We shouldn't expect much from a discount retailer, but some of the goods are cheap (vs. inexpensive) and check-out lines are slow.

Surprisingly, an airline did not appear on the Hall of Shame list until United Airlines checked in at #28.[10] Admittedly, the airline business has been a tough gig for decades. It's hard to earn profits in such a highly regulated, competitive, weather-dependent, high-cost, and safety-conscious industry. However, a New York-to-Los Angeles trek in the not-so-friendly skies takes just as long today as it did at the dawning of the commercial jet age in the 1960s, with no improvement in creature comforts. Planes are packed full and baggage fees are common. The disrespectful practice of overbooking continues. And while we should rejoice at the airlines recent consistency with regards to profitability, the industry has been reluctant to pass on fuel cost savings to its precious customer cargo.

Fortunately, there are several firms that score well on customer service metrics. Companies with the lowest percentage of "poor" scores in the 24/7 Wall St. survey included Bed Bath & Beyond, Amazon, Barnes & Noble, Marriott, and Auto Zone. When accentuating the positive by looking at firms recording the highest percentage of "excellent" ratings (which dictates placement in the 24/7 Wall St. Hall of *Fame*), the top performers were Amazon with 59.4 percent, Chick-fil-A with 47 percent, Apple with 40 percent, Marriott with 39.2 percent, and the grocery giant Kroger rounded out the top five with a 38.6 percent excellent rating.[11] When customers get what they expect, or maybe get a little more, they are generally satisfied. Expectations matter a great deal.

The Customer Satisfaction-Performance Paradox

We have all heard how satisfied customers are the keys to business success. However, a review of the research often tells a different story. A 2014 *MIT Sloan Management Review* piece outlined several studies and markets showing weak satisfaction scores for top-performing companies. Examples include mass market brands like McDonald's and Walmart. The article's authors, led by Timothy Keiningham, point to contributing factors such as a diverse customer set, low price requirements, convenience, and a large assortment of goods. Smaller firms are more likely to score higher in customer satisfaction since they cater to specific needs in focused niches. The data showed that higher market shares often have an inverted relationship to customer satisfaction. As for profits, the authors remarked, "While customer satisfaction and profitability are not mutually exclusive, they don't have to be aligned, either."[12]

Using a massive data set containing over 160,000 customer responses and performance metrics from 137 public firms, Keiningham and his colleagues found the importance of customer satisfaction is relative to competitors in a firm's category. Many firms experience either weak or negative return on investments from their satisfaction efforts. A company may unwittingly put pleasing unprofitable customers ahead of profits. Additionally, in explaining the relationship between customer satisfaction and customer spending, the researchers commented that "Changes in customers' satisfaction levels explain less than 1% of the variation in changes in their share of category spending. Yes, the relationship is statistically significant, but it is not very managerially relevant."[13]

The American Customer Satisfaction Index (ACSI) tracks consumers' general level of satisfaction. The ACSI recently went down for the eighth straight quarter and is at its lowest point in 10 years. Interestingly, the index tends to drop as unemployment goes down. Administrators of the ACSI gather that service employees may work more diligently and be more customer-centric in times of job scarcity. Also, stagnant wages may contribute to consumers' feelings of low satisfaction given that their earnings have not outpaced even low levels of inflation.[14]

Writing for *Bloomberg* in 2013, Eric Chemi used ACSI data for a sobering piece titled, "Proof That It Pays To Be America's Most Hated Companies." Chemi's analysis revealed "no statistical relationship between customer service scores and stock market returns." He further grumbled that airlines, banks, and cable and Internet providers "don't have much incentive to care" about customer service given the general contempt for customers by most major competitors in these industries.[15]

In addition to satisfaction, scholars use many other terms to describe how organizations interact with customers. Popular constructs for evaluating a firm's consideration of customers include marketing orientation; customer focus; customer-centric; customer orientation; customer driven; customer sensitive; and customer relationship management (CRM).[16] While the granddaddy of the terms is marketing orientation, CRM has become more hip since it is often the acronym used for the sales and marketing module of computerized enterprise systems that help run entire organizations. Later in the chapter I will specifically address the mis-named *relationship* portion of CRM for its superficiality.

Although there are differences in the terminology, suffice it to say that the aforementioned terms all deal with how a firm is geared toward treating the customer as a strategic or operational priority. For the sake of simplicity, our discussion will treat these terms as one. Much research indicates a positive relationship between market orientation factors and an organization's financial performance, but findings overall in this research domain are equivocal. Before citing a few specific studies, I invoke a challenge to conventional dogma surrounding market orientation with the following from Phil Rosenzweig, author of *The Halo Effect*:

> Just to be clear, I think that strong customer orientation probably does lead to better performance. Companies that listen to their customers, that design products and services to meet customer needs, and that work hard to satisfy their customers should, all else equal, outperform companies that don't. But you don't discover these companies by asking: Are you customer oriented? All you'll get is a self-reporting Halo, cued by company performance. If you want to measure customer orientation, you have to rely on measures that are independent of performance.[17]

Next, I present a small sampling of studies to illustrate how the degree of a firm's market orientation may influence organizational performance. First, a study of the hotel industry highlights how a firm's perception of its customers' values (e.g., price sensitivity, desire for services) will determine the type of orientation exhibited by the hotel. For example, if customers are considered more price sensitive, hotels will adopt a competitor orientation (i.e., match or beat competitor prices). Hotels with target customers that prize service are more likely to operate with both a customer orientation and a competitor orientation. Published in the *Journal of Business Research*, this study concluded that the stronger a firm's customer orientation efforts, the more the firm will demonstrate market advantages due to innovation and market differentiation.[18] Studies such as this tend to split hairs regarding how the firm reacts to external stimuli—be it customer or competitor activity. But this research raises an interesting question concerning high-end hotel customers (e.g., Ritz-Carlton patrons): To what degree is their hotel choice predicated on differentiated services versus the attractiveness of extraordinarily high prices (implying exclusivity)? As a two-time winner of the Malcolm Baldridge National Quality Award, Ritz-Carlton management would likely argue the answer lies in differentiation, quality, and customer satisfaction.[19]

A study of 434 Chinese manufacturing firms examined the *customer focus* component of the total quality management (TQM) approach for prioritizing activities of the firm. The study author concluded that customer relationship practices have a positive effect on production performance and, to a lesser extent, customer satisfaction and financial performance. While I am generally a strong proponent of TQM practices, the self-reporting aspect of customer orientation reported in the study's methodology is problematic. The data collection tool assesses customer orientation by asking respondents to rate their own firm on the following prompts: "Our company emphasizes the importance of customer orientation;" along with "We make every effort to understand our target customers;" and "We take our customers' opinions and suggestions seriously." Managers' positive biases will likely present themselves when answering *Agree* or *Strongly Agree* to these questions.[20]

Another example from the literature is a meta-study published in the *Journal of Marketing* that compiled 114 separate studies. The authors concluded that "the market orientation-performance relationship is stronger in samples of manufacturing firms, in low power-distance and uncertainty avoidance cultures, and in studies that use subjective measures of performance."[21] This conditional interpretation of outcomes is indicative of the difficulty with generalizing results of this phenomenon to broader populations. While our intuition may lead us to believe a strong marketing orientation (i.e., customer focus) will translate into better financial results, the findings from the academic literature are not so clear or convincing.

It's All About Relationships

Marketers have been moving away from relying on transaction-oriented interactions with customers—or at least the appearance of that cold reality. Relationships have been all the rage in marketing circles for the last couple of decades. As I stated previously, CRM modules are standard elements of firms' IT infrastructures and enterprise systems. Numerous cloud-based services offer impressive capabilities to store, retrieve, and configure customer data. This data represents a strategically important resource for ongoing customer analysis, targeting, follow-up, and promotional initiatives. For example, while I could care less about my car dealer sending me a "Happy Birthday" e-mail, I do appreciate the occasional special discount offer, recall notice, or reminder for maintenance.

But *relationship* is a strong word. It implies trust and some level of reciprocity, a two-way street that goes beyond the simple exchange of fees for goods or services. Conversely, *transaction* is such a cold, impersonal term. Relationship is much warmer and evokes the emotional connection coveted by marketers. If you have a romantic, family, friendly, or even just a professional relationship with someone, you expect intelligible and prompt responses when you call or interact. Below are a few examples of some less-than-stellar responses (and often no response) that I have received from firms that have been doing well in the marketplace.

Hanes not-so-tighty-whiteys: I sent Hanes Brands a detailed letter with several tags and waistbands of Hanes Men's Briefs that had lost their elasticity. The briefs must have hit their mean-time-to-failure because several of them failed around the same time. I received no response from the company after one year, plenty of time to investigate what had happened. Although the items were far from new, I deserved at least a *brief*, cursory reply.

Brews you could lose: I sent the Boston Beer Company a letter recounting an unsatisfying experience I had with a case of Sam Adams Boston Lager. Despite my sending them a detailed letter and the lot numbered portion of the box, I did not get a response.

Frozen dinner: Let it go! I wrote to Weight Watcher's after opening a Smart Ones frozen dinner that was compromised. The clear plastic that covers the meal was torn, likely due to excess adhesive used on the outer carton. Photocopies of the packaging, with lot numbers, were included with my detailed letter. It's been over a year now and I'm still waiting for a response. I just can't *let it go*.

Not the best fit: I asked my local gym (a small regional chain named Best Fitness) to reduce my membership dues to the minimum rate since

I was no longer using premium services or multiple locations. They said, "Sure, but . . ." I would have to quit and rejoin the gym, which gave them the legal right to extort an additional $49.99 from me for reinitiation alms! Bear in mind that I had been a member in good standing for six years, a nice long relationship, I thought. Gyms in general have a reputation for being sales-oriented and not member-centric. This particular organization is strictly sales driven and does a nice business mainly due to clean, convenient locations. As a customer, I needed to realize that this company was more structured around the mantra *Customer prospect is king*. Existing customers unwilling to be upsold additional services were not a priority. This *relationship* ended amicably because I realized we had different goals. I told them it wasn't me that was the problem—it was them! I now understand that the gym's focus is new business. I just wish they were more upfront about it.

Victoria has a dirty little secret: Here is the response my wife received after she submitted a complaint to Victoria's Secret for shipping the wrong colored sweater, which was also poorly packaged:

Dear Leanne,

Thank you for taking the time to write a review and share your feedback. It is my privilege to respond to you personally. I appreciate you telling us about your experience in regard to the quality and packaging on your recent order. I assure you that I have personally shared your comments with the appropriate team. We truly value your opinion and your voice has been heard.

Our customer feedback often provides us with direction for future merchandise and services. I would like to invite you to come back and post more of your feedback, now that our Ratings and Reviews have gone live on our website. We look forward to seeing your feedback on your future purchases! Leanne, you've chosen Victoria's Secret and we think of that as a privilege. If there's *anything more we can do for you* [emphasis mine] please email or call us any time.

Not to be picky, but saying "anything more we can do" implies they have already done something—which they had not. Victoria's Secret Customer Service thinks that the above e-mail signifies a resolution. It's a typical example of a patronizing response meant to convey false empower-ment onto a customer desperate for attention and closure. In the end, it took two long phone calls and supervisory intervention to rectify the error.

The short vignettes presented above are part of a much longer list of which I will not subject you to (you're welcome!). Nearly everyone has similar tales to tell. Yet, the optimist in me is compelled to share a couple of instances where companies possessed a strong grasp of marketing ori-entation, meaning they consciously did their best to attend to customer feedback, including:

> Devil Dog heaven: My young daughter went through a demonic phase where she worshipped Drake's Devil Dog Devil's Food Cakes. One day she thought the product tasted funny, and sure enough the box proclaimed "New Great Taste." It was indeed new, but not great. We called Drake's and were told that the company chefs had tested the new recipe and people *loved it*. We stopped buying them immediately. A few months later Drakes sent us a letter, with coupons for free products, stating "thanks to loyal cus-tomers like you" the company was reverting back to the old recipe!

> Coffee cream bliss: Nestle committed a similar faux paus when they altered the formula for their Coffee-mate product. This decision dra-matically changed the aftertaste of the flavored coffee creams. Again, I called, was told about the wonderful results from test marketing, and stopped buying. Apparently other customers felt the same way because a few months later a nice letter, accompanied by more cou-pons, arrived stating they were going back to the old formula.

While these examples may seem trivial, each firm's willingness to lis-ten to customers and admit mistakes likely saved the product lines from extinction. Self-advocacy among customers should be an important part of our consumer culture. Marketers need the feedback especially when they don't ask for it. Note that many formal market research projects are positively biased, seeking to confirm management's perceptions and tactics. Unsolicited customer feedback need not be reserved for negative experiences. Consumers should contact marketers when they have good experiences as well as bad ones. After all, healthy relationships require ongoing communication. A customer's independence ultimately hinges on the free will to enter into and opt out of transactions and relationships.

Buyer Beware

We all realize organizations need to operate in the black. For-profit firms are in business to make money and enhance shareholder value. Not-for-profits desire a surplus to continue their missions. But relentless, short-term financial pressures can yield some questionable tactics and bad organizational behavior. For instance:

> Package size matters: A simple ruse perpetrated by many pack-aged food companies involves the clandestine act of package size reduction. One can sympathize with producers when the cost of goods and logistics rise, leading to price increases for end-users. Consumers don't like this reality but accept it nonetheless. However, many firms reduce package contents *and* raise prices, thereby double dipping into the budgets and vulnerability of con-sumers. The worst part, despite the relationship puffery and our supposed socioeconomic contract with these firms, consumers are not informed of *New, Reduced Volume.* Loyal customers are not forewarned with coupons, new labeling or field merchandising specialists that scream, "Get Less for Your Dollar." Consumers are only told when packages get bigger, unless of course the smaller portions are in the customer's best interest (e.g., lower calorie serv-ings or convenient travel sizes).

Some displeasing examples of stealth downsizing schemes committed by popular brands, reported by business journalist Douglas McIntyre, in-clude: The extra-large Snickers Bar was cut into two pieces so it is "easier to share," but the total amount of candy bar is reduced by 11 percent with no price change; Tropicana Orange Juice, in order to compensate for higher costs from a damaging frost, reduced their half-gallon from 64 oz to 59 oz (an 8-percent reduction). It still looks like a half-gallon until you read the fine print; Haagen-Dazs ice cream revamped the pint-sized container by shedding 12.5 percent of the contents, but cleverly retained the same cover; and PepsiCo's Frito-Lay reduced the family-size bag of chips from 16 oz to 14 oz.[22]

Albacore tuna brand Chicken of the Sea dramatically trimmed its 6-oz can down to a 5-oz can (nearly a 17-percent reduction) as a way to deal with higher tuna costs. Additional offenders of surreptitious content shrinkage include Kraft Foods' Saltines, Kellogg's cereals, Hershey's Reese's minis and miniatures, Proctor & Gamble's Bounty paper towels, and Heinz Ketchup. I do not begrudge any of these firms their right to raise prices and earn profits, but an ethical dilemma exists when loyal customers are not informed of diminished value. If marketers desire a relationship, they should behave and communicate as though they are in one.[23]

Self-service tsunami: Consumers have grown accustomed to pumping their own gas and doing much of their own banking either online or via automatic teller machines (ATMs). Self-service check-outs are more common at retail establishments. Self-assembly of furniture and other fixtures, courtesy of firms like IKEA, continues to convert passive consumers into do-it-yourself subcontractors. Worth checking out is Craig Lambert's 2015 book *Shadow Work: The Unpaid, Unseen Jobs That Fill Your Day*. Lambert provides an insightful account of work that has migrated to consumers.[24] There is indeed a fine line between customer exploitation and customer empowerment.

Surge pricing: Also referred to as dynamic and discriminatory pricing, surge pricing makes economic sense from a supply and demand perspective. Peak demand times—be they for Uber cars, airplane seats, or electricity—command higher prices. This alleviates shortages since suppliers will get into the game if above average profits can be had. However, surge pricing tends to penalize customers (some of which are very loyal) during peak gouging times. *Customer is prey* may be a more appropriate axiom during high points in demand cycles. Much deserved margins for sellers can quickly deteriorate into a customer perception of profiteering.

Loyalty programs based on customer dollars spent tend to lessen the negative impact of surge pricing on loyal customers. For example,

Southwest Airlines' loyalty program dispenses points to customers based on dollars spent, not miles flown. Marriott Hotels, known for its popular Rewards Program, recently instituted lower pricing for members in an attempt to book more customers directly through its own channels versus third-party travel sites.

> Contracts, warranties, and rebates: Purchase agreement contracts are proof that a pleasant customer experience is not the top priority of many firms. Cell phone and credit card agreements, akin to the paperwork required of a 30-year mortgage, are prime examples of this contractual malaise. How many customers can attest to have actually read one of these legal tomes? Firms have relied on the fine print of contracts to impart arbitration language to eliminate the chances of class action lawsuits.[25] Consumers often don't realize that arbitration clauses are buried in many of the contracts they sign, negating their opportunity for a day in court. A *New York Times* investigation into a sample of federal cases filed between 2010 and 2014 revealed that "of 1,179 class actions that companies sought to push into arbitration, judges ruled in their favor in four out of every five cases."[26] However, in 2016 the Consumer Financial Protection Bureau ruled that financial institutions will once again have to permit banking customers the right to file suit.[27]

Incidentally, consumers' attitudes toward business contracts may be part of the problem. Uriel Haran of Ben-Gurion University suggests that a "contract's moral component is weighted more heavily for individuals than for organizations." Haran's research revealed a contract breach by individuals is viewed like a broken promise, or "moral transgression," while the same violation by an organization (i.e., corporate personhood) is considered a "legitimate business decision." For example, participants were asked to rate the cancelling of a home renovation contract by a contracting firm because the firm could make more money on another job. The contract breach by an individual home renovator (e.g., sole proprietor) received more severe ratings of immorality and greed than the breach committed by a contractor perceived as a company (i.e., not a sole individual). Our courts of law may consider corporations to be people, but consumers appear to morally judge real people in a harsher manner than corporations.[28]

Extended warranties, with their limitations on merchant liability, are essentially insurance premiums for devices whose time-to-failure is largely known beforehand by producers. The purchase of a warranty may lower a consumer's sense of risk and the probability for post purchase cognitive dissonance. However, warranties are more advantageous for the seller due to stipulations lurking in the fine print, arduous redemption procedures, and failure by consumers to act.

And then there is the most diabolical of discounts: the rebate. Appearing as promotional eye candy, the rebate is often a chore to apply for and essentially delays the fulfillment of a promised discount. Rebates from pharmaceutical firms entail one of the more vexing aspects of our convoluted health care system. Due to rising deductibles, many families pay the entire cost for pricey medications, yet the insurance company often gets a rebate from the drug manufacturer—even though the insurer didn't pay anything![29] While the insurance company may be treated royally in these instances, it's serf city for the lowly insured.

Oddly, the rebate is one of the more straightforward line items you encounter when buying a car. Dealers are very explicit when informing buyers that the manufacturer's rebate goes directly to the dealership. Yet despite this outlier of transparency, traditional car buying and its requisite haggling endure to produce unpleasant mismatches between professional sellers and amateur buyers. Even confident car buyers need to grasp that a busy auto dealership sells in a day what the average consumer buys in a lifetime.

Truth in advertising: Although consumers benefit greatly from competition among firms, this can lead to unscrupulous marketing tactics designed to help brands stand out from all the marketing noise and advertising clutter. You may recall the campaign for the Shape-Up toning sneakers from Skechers USA, Inc. The ads claimed the shoe would help wearers lose weight and tone up the muscles in their butt, legs, and abdomen. The ads were so effective that even the Federal Trade Commission (FTC) noticed. After being charged by the FTC, Skechers agreed to pay $40 million in 2012 for customer refunds.[30] Similar charges by the FTC against

Reebok in 2011 led to that company agreeing to pay $25 million for deceptive advertising.[31]

National retailer Lord & Taylor got into hot water with the FTC over an aggressive social media campaign in 2015. According to an FTC press release, the company "gave 50 fashion influencers a free Paisley Asymmetrical Dress and paid them between $1,000 and $4,000 each to post a photo of themselves wearing it on Instagram or another social media site." The company preapproved all the online posts. Lord & Taylor also paid for and edited an article about the dress that appeared in an online fashion magazine. There was no disclosure in these promotions indicating that the company was supporting the online social content. Jessica Rich, Director of the FTC's Bureau of Consumer Protection, stated, "Lord & Taylor needs to be straight with consumers in its online marketing campaigns. Consumers have the right to know when they're looking at paid advertising."[32] Amen to that.

The examples and data that I have shared reflect a reality that customers need to be diligent and self-advocate. While most customers are not treated like kings, they have the right to challenge sellers and to expect a fair, reasonable value. Customers must let marketers know whether expectations have been met or not, and manage their own expectations. Finally, if you are lucky enough to feel as though you are being treated like a king—enjoy it!

Contra Maxims for Customer Interaction

Only the best customers are kings. Buyers and sellers should transact like they are in real relationships. It's all about an exchange of value. Good customer service requires listening and action. Customer service: it's often nothing personal—it's just business. Customer service *can* be a great differentiator.

Notes

1. Kelly Tian and Bill Keep, *Customer Fraud and Business Responses: Let the Marketer Beware* (Westport, CT: Quorum, 2002).

2. Sam Stebbins, "Customer Service Hall of Shame," *24/7 Wall St*, 23 Jul 2015, http://247wallst.com/special-report/2015/07/23/customer-service-hall-of-fame-2/4/ (accessed Apr 14, 2016).

3. Direct TV, "AT&T to Acquire Direct TV," 18 May 2014, http://news.directv.com/2014/05/18/directv-att-merger-press-release/ (accessed Apr 25, 2016).

4. Glassdoor, Inc., "Dish Network Employee Reviews," 2016, https://www.glassdoor.com/Reviews/dish-network-reviews-SRCH_KE0,12.htm (accessed May 6, 2016).

5. Gautham Nagesh and Thomas Gryta, "FCC to Fine AT&T $100 Million Over Capping Unlimited Data Plans," *The Wall Street Journal*, 17 Jun 2015, http://www.wsj.com/articles/fcc-to-fine-at-t-100-million-for-capping-unlimited-data-plans-1434557988 (accessed Apr 25, 2016).

6. Stebbins, "Customer Service Hall of Shame"

7. Ibid.

8. Ibid., Market capitalizations and return on equity percentages are from Morningstar Equity Analyst Reports dated from February 3 to April 21, 2016.

9. Tom Springer, Charles Kim, Frederic Debruyne, Domenico Azzarello and Jeff Melton, "Breaking the Back of Customer Churn," Bain & Company, Inc., 2014, 2, http://bain.com/Images/BAIN_BRIEF_Breaking_the_back_of_customer_churn.pdf (accessed Apr 22, 2016).

10. Stebbins, "Customer Service Hall of Shame"

11. Michael Sauter, Samuel Stebbins and Thomas Frohlich, "Customer Service Hall of Fame," 2015b, http://247wallst.com/special-report/2015/07/23/customer-service-hall-of-fame-2/4/ (accessed Apr 22, 2016).

12. Timothy Keiningham, Sunil Gupta, Lerzan Aksoy and Alexander Buoye, "The High Price of Customer Satisfaction," *MIT Sloan Management Review*, 18 Mar 2014, http://sloanreview.mit.edu/article/the-high-price-of-customer-satisfaction/?use_credit=a2cb4cbee5d6634c4c73ab1e333b3772 (accessed May 6, 2016).

13. Ibid.

14. American Customer Satisfaction Index, LLC., "National ASCI Q4 2015: ASCI: Downturn in National Customer Satisfaction Reaches Eight Consecutive Quarters," LLC., 29 Mar 2016, http://www .theacsi.org/news-and-resources/press-releases/press-2016/press-release-national-acsi-q4-2015 (accessed May 6, 2016).

15. Eric Chemi, "Proof that it Pays to be America's Most Hated Companies," Bloomberg L.P., 18 Dec 2013, http://www.bloomberg.com/news/articles/2013-12-17/proof-that-it-pays-to-be-americas-most-hated-companies (accessed May 17, 2016).

16. Shaohan Cai, "The Importance of Customer Focus For Organizational Performance: A Study of Chinese Companies," *International Journal of Quality & Reliability Management* 26, no. 4 (2009): 369–379.

17. Phil Rosenzweig, *The Halo Effect and Eight Other Business Delusions that Deceive Managers* (New York, NY: Free Press, 2014), 72.

18. Kevin Zhou, James Brown and Chekitan Dev, "Market Orientation, Competitive Advantage, and Performance: A Demand-based Perspective," *Journal of Business Research* 62, no. 11 (2009): 1063–1070.

19. NIST, U.S. Department of Commerce, "Malcolm Baldridge National Quality Award, 1999 Award Recipient, Service Category," 15 Feb 2000, http://www.nist.gov/baldrige/ritz.cfm (accessed May 25, 2016). Note: Ritz-Carlton won the Baldridge Award in 1992 and 1999. Ritz-Carlton became an independently operated division of Marriott International, Inc. in 1997.

20. Cai, "The Importance of Customer Focus"

21. Ahmet Kirca, Satish Jayachandran and William Bearden, "Market Orientation: A Meta-analytic Review and Assessment of its Antecedents and Impact on Performance," *Journal of Marketing* 69, no. 2 (2005): 24–41.

22. Douglas McIntyre, "U.S. Companies Shrink Packages as Food Prices Rise" *Daily Finance*, 11 Apr 2011, http://www.dailyfinance.com/2011/04/04/u-s-companies-shrink-packages-as-food-prices-rise/ (accessed Apr 25, 2016).

23. Ibid.

24. Craig Lambert, *Shadow Work: The Unpaid, Unseen Jobs That Fill Your Day* (Berkeley, CA: Counterpoint, 2015).

25. Andrew Pincus, "The Advantages of Arbitration," *New York Times*, 24 May 2012, http://dealbook.nytimes.com/2012/05/24/the-advantages-of-arbitration/?_r=0 (accessed May 7, 2016).

26. Jessica Silver-Greenberg and Robert Gebeloff, "Arbitration Everywhere, Stacking the Deck of Justice," *The New York Times*, 31 Oct 2015, http://www.nytimes.com/2015/11/01/business/dealbook/arbitration-everywhere-stacking-the-deck-of-justice.html (accessed May 6, 2016).

27. Jessica Silver-Greenberg and Michael Corkery, "Rule on Arbitration Would Restore Right to Sue Banks," *New York Times*, 5 May 2016, http://www.nytimes.com/2016/05/05/business/dealbook/consumer-agency-moves-to-assert-bank-customers-right-to-sue.html (accessed May 6, 2016).

28. Uriel Haran, "A Person-organization Discontinuity in Contract Perception: Why Corporations Can Get Away with Breaking Contracts but Individuals Cannot," *Management Science* 59, no. 12 (2013): 2837–2853.

29. Robert Langreth, "Your Prescription Gets a Rebate—for Insurers," *Bloomberg Businessweek*, Oct 10–16, 2016, 23–24.

30. Federal Trade Commission, "Skechers Will Pay $40 million to Settle FTC Charges that it Deceived Consumers with Ads for 'Toning Shoes,'" 16 May 2012, https://www.ftc.gov/news-events/press-releases/2012/05/skechers-will-pay-40-million-settle-ftc-charges-it-deceived (accessed May 8, 2016).

31. Federal Trade Commission, "Reebok to Pay $25 million in Customer Refunds to Settle FTC Charges of Deceptive Advertising of EasyTone and RunTone Shoes," 28 Sep 2011, https://www.ftc.gov/news-events/press-releases/2011/09/reebok-pay-25-million-customer-refunds-settle-ftc-charges (accessed May 8, 2016).

32. Federal Trade Commission, "Lord & Taylor Settles FTC Charges it Deceived Consumers Through Paid Article in an Online Fashion Magazine and Paid Instagram Posts by 50 'Fashion Influencers,'" 15 Mar 2015, https://www.ftc.gov/news-events/press-releases/2016/03/lord-taylor-settles-ftc-charges-it-deceived-consumers-through (accessed May 8, 2016).

CHAPTER 3

People are Our Most Important Asset

Organizations are too often prisons for the human soul.
—Charles Handy, Foreword of *Organizing Genius*

We called for workers, but people came.
—Max Frisch, Swiss author, referring to
European guest worker programs

Arguably the most condescending of the maxims deconstructed in this book is the proclamation that *People are our most important asset*. Institutionally self-serving, this declaration takes many semantic forms and is by no means used sparingly. An array of corporate communication tools lauds the power of the people behind successful ventures and products. All hail those on the front lines servicing customers and providing solutions in the field. Executives praise associates, team members, staff, and rank and file as critical parts of one big corporate family. People are the glue. They make the organization hum, click, go, and outduel competitors. Sometimes, albeit rarely, these sentiments are genuine.

Unfortunately, the false praise heaped on an organization's personnel is frequently used to co-opt public opinion and appease unhappy, perishable employees. It is often politically correct lip service spouted by senior managers far removed from these living, breathing *assets*. Indeed, aside from being rolled up into the intangible assets or goodwill component of a business valuation (e.g., in the case of an acquisition), employees are very seldom accounted for as assets in financial accounting. Over 20 years ago management sage Charles Handy scribed, "For a long time now, corporate chairmen have been saying that their real assets were their people, but few really meant it and none went so far as to put those assets on their balance sheets."[1] A survey published in 2012 asked 180 accounting professionals the following hypothetical question: Should human capital be accounted for and reported on the balance sheet? Only 13 percent responded affirmatively, with 87 percent answering no. Subjectivity and difficulty with measuring the value of human capital were common reasons given for responding in the negative.[2] Nevertheless, employees do materialize on the books as direct labor costs and general and administrative (G&A) expenses.

Before proceeding I must make the following distinction: Most firms view their products (and services), intellectual property (IP), business models, and shareholders as more important than the bulk of their employee assets. The best workers and managers will be hard pressed to succeed without solid products, systems, and brands. Relatedly, Jeffrey Pfeffer and Robert Sutton of Stanford's Graduate School of Business noted that "Great systems are often more important than great people."[3] However, isn't it common to think that *people* are necessary to create and contribute within these systems? Yes, but once products, business models, and systems are established, I contend that *most* employees are considered less critical than those factors that are the focus of the enterprise. I do not qualify or trivialize this proposition as *nothing personal*, but instead acknowledge it is a matter of the strategy and performance metrics that drive a typical firm's behavior. Believe me, as an employee myself, I take no pleasure in this realization.

Let's look at a few examples. You could replace nearly everyone at Facebook, yet its flagship social networking site would likely continue to perform adequately in the marketplace for some time. Facebook's market strength and network effects dwarf the value provided by the bulk of the company's current employees. Given Facebook's sizable financial assets, it is more likely to acquire its next blockbuster product than develop it organically. In matters of a technology or company acquisitions, Facebook would rely on select employees to accomplish any deals (e.g., those with discovery, valuation, and due diligence skills).

Likewise, and hypothetically, Alphabet's Google would continue to dominate the search business in the near term even if the majority of its employees' work were outsourced. The legacy of the restructured Alphabet will likely showcase its business model—which yes, contains a people component—as more vital to organizational performance than the majority of its employees. With the exception of a subset of key people with particular skills, knowledge, and vision, most employees are replaceable. In practice, this is how many organizations view their employees.

Importantly, many tech workers at Facebook and Alphabet are more valuable in the new knowledge economy due to their specific and relatively scarce skill sets. Research and development organizations also contain many vital employees. On a larger scale, employees at service-intensive businesses such as package delivery concerns (e.g., United Parcel Service drivers and handlers) and hotels (e.g., housekeepers at Hilton) are critical to daily operations. However, these semi-skilled employees are only vital from the standpoint that they are organized and able to collectively walk off the job.

Suppose a firm decides to outsource production of a long successful product. Many may think this decision is a mistake—losing tribal and tacit knowledge, the idiosyncrasies of the process, and application of secret sauce that only comes from years of experience. The original crew that made the products was excellent, but as the product line matures, in-house manufacturing may no longer be strategically aligned. The new subcontractor is good enough. The firm gives up some control in exchange for headcount reduction and cost savings. Note that I am not condoning rampant outsourcing but merely conveying its reality. Outsourcing is often a short-sighted remedy resulting in the permanent loss of internal competencies.

Consider the aforementioned term *headcount*. It's a convenient way of categorizing employees into a neat unit of measure, like SKUs (stock keeping units). Each employee exists as a unique yet impersonal part number. Many dutiful workers cling to the fairytale of a social contract between employee and organization. Yet even the concept of an *employee* has a short history. Noted management author Gary Hamel bristles with the following perspective:

One doesn't have to be a Marxist to be awed by the scale and success of early-20th-century efforts to transform strong-willed human beings into docile employees. The demands of the modern industrial workplace required a dramatic resculpting of human habits and values. To sell one's time rather than what one produced, to pace one's work to the clock, to eat and sleep at precisely defined intervals, to spend long days endlessly repeating the same, small task—none of these were, or are, natural human instincts. It would be dangerous, therefore, to assume that the concept of "the employee"— or any other tenet in the creed of modern management—is anchored on the bedrock of eternal truth.[4]

The philosopher John Locke weighed in on labor's contribution over three centuries ago with, "For 'tis labor indeed that puts the difference of value on everything."[5] An astute observation for its time and still relevant today. Manual labor, thoughtful analysis, creativity, and human decision making still produce value, yet the truly differentiating producers of significant value are a small minority of all those employed.

My apologies for beginning this chapter with a bit of gloom and doom. I promise I'll provide some positivity later in the chapter. My point here is not to depress you but to awaken you. Your job and career are *your* responsibility. The majority of employees will be vulnerable to career flux and displacement. If organizations can reduce costs by limiting headcount, that is exactly what they will do. You are likely *not* your employer's most important asset!

No Labor of Love

A Gallup poll measuring the engagement of U.S. workers has received a lot of attention for its consistency and sobering depiction of the workplace. For the past 15 years, Gallup reports less than one-third of workers in the United States have reported being engaged on the job. Gallup considers an engaged employee to be "involved in, enthusiastic about, and committed to their work or workplace."[6] Note that disengaged does not necessarily mean ineffective. Many a miserable employee is still pretty darn good at what they do—they just are not enthusiastic about doing it. However, the level of disaffection in the U.S. workforce is alarming given how we spend so much of our lives at work.

Furthermore, Gallup reports the worldwide figure outside the United States for those occupationally engaged is a woeful 13 percent.[7] A recent Conference Board publication commented on the ramifications of this lack of engagement with, "Employees cannot be brand ambassadors and advocates if they are disengaged."[8] Indeed, a 2015 report by the global consulting firm Deloitte revealed that "Upwards of half the workforce would not recommend their employer to their peers."[9] Relatedly *The Economist*, citing survey data from the consultancy Accenture, reported that:

> 31% of employees don't like their boss, 32% were actively looking for a new job, and 43% felt that they received no recognition for their work. The biggest problem with trying to do more with less is that you can end up turning your sheep into wolves—and your biggest resources into your biggest liabilities.[10]

Still another report from Deloitte, surveying over 7,000 business leaders and human resources (HR) managers in 130 countries, revealed 85 percent of respondents ranked employee engagement as a top priority. However, just "46 percent of companies report they are ready to tackle the engagement challenge."[11] Equally disturbing is the nonchalance with which we digest these figures. Misery is largely absorbed as an unconscious given by today's worker bees and harried managers. The consistency of survey results indicates disengagement is the norm.

Additional data from the Society of Human Resource Management (SHRM), reported in 2015, point to still more discontent in the workplace. Six-hundred respondents revealed what factors were "very important" to them with regard to job satisfaction. The top four aspects (out of 43 in total) were respectful treatment of all employees at all levels (72 percent); trust between employees and senior management (64 percent); benefits (63 percent); and compensation (61 percent). When later queried on their own *level of satisfaction* with these aspects, they responded "very satisfied" in only one-third or less of the cases (i.e., 33, 28, 27, and 24 percent, respectively).[12]

A Harris Interactive Poll found 73 percent of employees surveyed reported feeling stressed at work. The leading contributor to the stress was low pay, narrowly beating out several other gripes (i.e., coworkers, commute, and workload).[13]

The chronically disengaged, underemployed, and unemployed are eerily akin to the zombie genre's undead moniker. Even with official unemployment rates at historically low levels in the United States, nearly two million have dropped out of the workforce and are not included in government figures. *Bloomberg Businessweek* reports the level of discouragement is worse in the Euro Zone with over 11 million not looking for work.[14] The polarization of the American job market has come about from massive job creation at the part-time, low wage, gig, and flexible end of the spectrum (e.g., fast food, hospitality, and car services) while the number of better compensated jobs decreases.

This vocational malaise is compounded by our culture's traditional view of work. Much of our identity and social currency are tied to our jobs. For instance, when meeting someone for the first time, it does not take long for one party to blurt out, "So, what do you do for a living?" As Charles Handy glumly observed, "We seem to have made work into a god and then made it difficult for many to worship."[15] Employee angst appears to be the rule rather than the exception. Dependent care demands, outsourcing, automation, and a decline in private sector labor unions have contributed to the growing anxiety of the American worker.

Wages have been relatively stagnant for decades, especially when compared to economic growth and corporate profits. The Bureau of Labor Statistics continues to report lower unemployment numbers *without* the expected rise in real wages.[16] Firms have done well managing the cost of HR but not the investment aspect of human capital. Steven Greenhouse, author of *The Big Squeeze: Tough Times for the American Worker*, laments how, "The share of corporate income going to workers has sunk to its lowest level since 1951."[17]

Greenhouse, the work and labor correspondent for *The New York Times*, documents a host of labor-related unpleasantries in *The Big Squeeze*, including time card manipulation by unscrupulous supervisors; off-the-clock work expectations placed on hourly employees; hostile work environments; locking in of overnight employees (e.g., Walmart's Sam's Club); and a litany of downsizing, rightsizing, outsourcing, and offshoring. Greenhouse also chronicles the drop in pensions in favor of 401(k) plans as well as increases in employee contributions for health care benefits. The growing use of independent contractors (e.g., FedEx Ground drivers and Uber drivers), temporary and permatemp workers, and illegal immigration's impact at the low end of the wage spectrum have all put downward pressure on wages.[18]

There is another boogeyman to reckon with when it comes to the lackluster gains in real wages—productivity growth.[19] George Mason University economics professor Tyler Cowen commented in March, 2016 that "Labor productivity [in the U.S.] has been growing at an average of only 1.3 percent annually since the start of 2005, compared with 2.8 percent annually in the preceding 10 years." Perhaps the bulk of productivity gains from the Internet and digitization were realized in the earlier years of the information age.[20] A Conference Board report in 2015 conveyed similar gloom with respect to productivity, claiming, "In the past seven years (2007–2014), the rise in the efficiency of global production has been reduced to about a quarter of what it was during the prior seven years (1999–2006), with little recovery in sight before 2025."[21] The report stressed the need for continuous improvement of worker skillsets in order for productivity rates to increase substantially.

Work like an Amazonian

It's easy to appreciate the accomplishments of Amazon founder and CEO Jeff Bezos, but it isn't easy to work for him. Infamous for high pressure white collar work environments as well as draconian treatment of warehouse workers, Amazon appears both refreshing and Dickensian. Refreshing for its brashness, results orientation, and accountability, but medieval for its harsh treatment of the so-called *most important asset*. Amazon's main strength is not product superiority or people en masse. Amazon's online retail business performs well due to dominant online branding supported by data-driven marketing and logistics productivity. A massive assortment of products is also critical to the firm's value proposition. The bulk of Amazon's people assets, meanwhile, are as disposable as a broken down fork truck in the warehouse.

Scathingly chronicled in a 2015 *New York Times* front page story, Amazon's demanding work culture is symptomatic of global competitive realities. Reporters Jodi Kantor and David Streitfeld claim the firm's high performance climate produces high employee turnover. Bezos sets a tone that challenges the status quo and encourages criticism of colleagues' suggestions. Yet stoked to the extreme, unidimensional Amazon employees end up unaffectionately referred to as *Amholes*.[22] Bezos appears to appreciate the value of human employees and sets about extracting as much of that value as is humanly possible. Most customers enjoying a good deal on an Amazon purchase may not approve of the firm's methods, but they will likely ignore the plight of those who got them their products so efficiently.

Some workers thrive in Amazon's go-getter culture. Yet Amazon's demanding meritocracy (a positive) reflects a hardboiled disposability not unlike that portrayed in Upton Sinclair's 1906 meat industry expose *The Jungle* (not so positive). *The Jungle's* main character, burly Lithuanian immigrant Jurgis Rudkus, excelled in the throughput-obsessed meatpacking complex until a workplace injury disenfranchised him on the merits of unbridled capitalism.[23]

Even with the allure of healthy performance bonuses, Amazon's work culture is not for everyone. For many it is a question of organizational fit. Bezos is unapologetic when discussing the culture at Amazon, writing in his 2016 Letter to Shareholders, "We never claim that our approach is the right one – just that it's ours – and over the last two decades, we've collected a large group of like-minded people. Folks who find our approach energizing and meaningful."[24] Similarly, the Jim Collins' classic *Good to Great* recounts the heyday and growth of Nucor Steel and its incentive-laden culture with the following: "Nucor rejected the old adage that people are your most important asset. In a good-to-great transformation, people are not your most important asset. The *right* people are."[25]

The early 20th century saw the rise of scientific management techniques championed by Frederick Winslow Taylor and the many disciples of the classical school of management thought. Often referred to as *Taylorism*, this was primarily a movement of industrial efficiency. Taylorism promoted piece rate incentives for workers, encouraged use of helpful fixtures and tools, optimized workflow, and implemented time and motion studies to improve throughput. However, Taylorism gets knocked (mostly unfairly) for treating workers like machines and not accounting for the human relations perspective. Today, scientific management principles continue to help increase productivity of workers and processes, resulting in improved competitiveness.

Alternatively, *The Economist* recently highlighted Taylorism's modern dark side, including the use of high tech measurement devices to monitor workers and their productivity—whether on site, on the road, or working from home. Workplace monitoring fits well with another weathered axiom, "what gets measured gets managed [done]."[26] *Harper's Magazine* published a report in 2015 arguing that electronic monitoring of workers adds undue stress and may decrease job performance. Heavy reliance on productivity metrics may result in wage theft—where supervisors get work done by employees who are not on the clock (e.g., before or after shifts, on breaks). The *Harper's* report cites a 2014 survey by Hart's Research that revealed 89 percent of fast food workers queried claimed they were victimized by wage theft at some level.[27] Wage theft is most likely to occur when managers are incentivized to keep labor costs at or below budget. Bear in mind many of these labor and expense budgets were likely pushed down onto the field supervisors charged with their compliance.

Harper's investigated the use of telematics for monitoring UPS drivers and their trucks, revealing demanding expectations for driver productivity. The report implies that telematics were introduced by management partly as a safety measure (e.g., seatbelt compliance, truck speeds, and whereabouts). However, *Harper's* describes UPS investor conference calls that tout the fleet's surveillance program as instrumental for operating efficiencies.[28] Paradoxically, the acknowledgement of all this monitoring somewhat weakens the argument against the maxim *People are our most important asset*. There certainly appears to be significant resources expended to ensure the efficient deployment of human capital in many firms—at least in businesses with significant labor costs. Again, perspective matters. Investors and operations managers view the data gleaned from surveillance as helpful. Meanwhile, the rank and file feel watched and overly scrutinized. This type of environment breeds ill will and mistrust between workers and management.

A 2015 study published in the journal *Management Science* probed the misconduct and productivity of workers at nearly 400 casual dining restaurants from five different firms. Researchers used "theft monitoring information technology" to measure worker theft and sales performance.

The study's authors reported "significant treatment effects in reduced theft and improved productivity that appear to be primarily driven by changed worker behavior rather than worker turnover." One of the drivers for the productivity increase was said to be workers' perception of "general oversight."[29] The study did not specifically mention employee attitudes toward the added surveillance.

A recent *McKinsey Quarterly* article postulated that millennials will be less bothered by monitoring in the workplace than older employees. Millennials have been voluntarily sharing intimate details about themselves for years online. However, privacy issues may steer data collection of employee activity toward "aggregated and anonymized (rather than individual) data."[30]

Domo Arigato, Mr. Roboto

A 2014 Pew Research Center survey asked nearly 1,900 experts the following query: Will networked, automated, artificial intelligence (AI) applications and robotic devices have displaced more jobs than they have created by 2025? The answer: 48 percent responded affirmatively while 52 percent felt technological advances will help create additional jobs. This result is a bit of a coin toss, and the survey is only asking for a prediction just over 10 years out. Many survey respondents see massive unemployment and bigger increases in income inequality in the future.[31]

Two Oxford scholars, Carl Frey and Michael Osborne, released a study in 2013 cataloguing the probability of 702 occupations being automated. Professions requiring significant finger dexterity and strong perception and cognition are safest from the cost savings promised by automation. These researchers also found a negative relationship between salary and the likelihood of being automated. Education level revealed a similar pattern. From their forward looking model, Frey and Osborne estimate that "47 percent of total U.S. employment is in the high risk category" and susceptible to being automated in roughly 10 to 20 years.[32]

In their recent book *The Second Machine Age*, MIT's Erik Brynjolfsson and Andrew McAfee declared that:

> There's never been a better time to be a worker with special skills
> or the right education, because these people can use technology

to create and capture value. However, there's never been a worse time to be a worker with only 'ordinary' skills and abilities to offer, because computers, robots, and other digital technologies are acquiring these skills and abilities at an extraordinary rate.[33]

Humans are better at nonstandard tasks, while computers do what they are told and excel at rule-based work, such as managing retirement accounts. Many investment funds are mandated to keep certain percentages in equities, bonds, and cash. With simple rules to follow, robo-advisers are seen as a perfect, low-cost solution for long-term investing. A human adviser may only be necessary to upsell products, persuade clients to invest more, or just function as a receptacle for client rage during periods of poor returns.[34]

A recent *New York Times Magazine* article on robo-advisers included the following comment from former Barclay's CEO Antony Jenkins, "I predict that the number of branches and people employed in the financial-services sector may decline by as much as 50 percent."[35] The good news is hopefully the cost to clients goes down. The bad news is obvious if the robo-adviser takes *your* job. To survive the oncoming purge, a human adviser will have to become more of a consultative seller of investment products rather than a transaction-oriented executor—that's the robot's responsibility.

Not surprisingly, Amazon has invested heavily in automation, including the 2012 acquisition of robot maker Kiva Systems for $775 million.[36] Additionally, companies such as Fetch and Harvest Automation have been pursuing the warehouse labor market with bin-toting bots that scoot alongside human stock pickers. According to *Bloomberg Businessweek*, these warehouse robots can be purchased outright for $15,000 to $25,000 or rented for as little as $1.40 per hour.[37]

Japan, long home to leading makers of factory robots, has made future advances in robotics a national priority. In addition to robots that cut down on labor costs for manufacturers, Japan is keen to develop automated personal aids and hospitality "workers." An aging population, shrinking labor force, a fascination with technology, and strong manufacturing base for robot componentry indicate future advances in Japanese robotics are likely. Conventional thinking usually exempts high-touch health care workers as replaceable via robots, but Japanese expertise and aging demographics may alter that mindset.[38]

In the early 1980s, I was a no-touch material handler in a midsized community hospital. Any material you could put on a cart—I handled it. It was a good job, except on every shift I had to deliver massive laundry carts to 10 nursing stations. It was like pushing reluctant elephants that dragged their feet. Too big to see around and too heavy to stop quickly if you were about to run over a patient or visitor (hospital staff knew enough to scatter). Short of putting two workers on each cart, this was a classic process in need of motorized augmentation. But alas, no mechanized assistance ever came to the rescue. For years I struggled with the great linen mammoths, comforted only by visions of Sinclair's Jurgis Rudkus in his slaughterhouse to give me perspective.

Automation has resulted in countless cases of improved efficiency, safety, and quality while reducing instances of backbreaking toil. My residential trash collection service is a good example. For years my municipality had three men on a truck until the service was outsourced to a private firm with a modern fleet (which had only two employees per truck). Now there is only one operator per truck; thanks to mechanical arms that effortlessly collect the trash. Service is much more efficient and workplace injuries have plummeted. The task is now accomplished faster, safer, and with fewer employees. It's progress, notwithstanding the job displacement.

People Get Ready...

Plenty of historical precedence suggests that I may be over-reacting to projected job losses as a result of advances in automation. Millions of displaced farm workers were absorbed into factory work during industrialization. The industrial revolution added jobs and helped improve quality of life in much of the world. Trains have proved to be a great boon to transportation efficiency. Cars and trucks replaced wagons and people on horseback, but the equine species endures.

However, globalization and the unprecedented pace of technological advances have put us in a more anxious state regarding the future of work and management. The market seeks the most cost efficient means of innovation and production. A massive number of jobs will likely disappear in the coming decades. Society will need coping strategies. Some of these strategies will not involve traditional jobs, or jobs at all. A parallel can be drawn to the Works Progress Administration (WPA) created to put people to work during the Great Depression, only this time we may be responding to the Great Automation.

MIT's Erik Brynjolfsson and Andrew McAfee offer some suggestions (not necessarily endorsements) for dealing with changes in the employment landscape, including the following:

- Product labeling that reads *MADE BY HUMANS*. In the spirit of the organic food, union label, and *buy American* campaigns, perhaps consumers will be inclined to buy products with a certified human touch.
- Government make-work and employment programs like the Depression-era Civil Conservation Corps.
- Investment in technology that assists human workers versus innovation seeking to replace humans.
- "Vouchers for basic necessities," and variations of guaranteed income for those not working.[39]

Related to the above suggestions, there is a movement centered in the United Kingdom promoting a 21-hour full-time workweek. Championed by the New Economics Foundation, the program intends to address social justice (i.e., fuller employment and HR), natural resources and sustainability, and economic markets.[40]

Since 2000 France has fiddled with a program that mandates a 35-hour week. The intent of this initiative is to increase employment with an annualization of working hours to accommodate business fluctuations. The French government and industry continue to tweak the program, but results have been mixed.[41] A potential benefit of these and other *less hours-less unemployment* schemes is knowledge. These experiments may help policy makers and industry leaders craft responses to unemployment resulting from advances in automation. But as many labor laws in Europe have demonstrated, if you make it too difficult or expensive to furlough workers, industry will resist hiring.[42]

There have been many positive exceptions to conventional people management regimens. In *The Future of Management*, Gary Hamel points to exemplars Google, Whole Foods, and W.L. Gore. Google fosters an experimental culture, discretionary use of time, high bonus potential, small teams, and lots of peer feedback. Whole Foods instills employee empowerment coupled with accountability, team-based bonus compensation, and a transparent *no-secrets* management philosophy. Lastly, W.L. Gore promotes self-selection for team assignments, flexible *dabble time*, peer-review employee appraisals, and a high-trust low-fear work climate.[43]

A model employer in retail is Costco. The firm is routinely praised for its consistent productivity and relatively high wages. *Fortune* reports Costco's employee turnover at 10 percent, a pittance compared to the retail industry average of 55 percent. The company claims longer employee tenure results in better customer service. Costco is ranked #1 among specialty retailers and #16 overall on *Fortune's* World's Most Admired Top 50 All-Stars.[44]

Vineet Nayar, CEO of Indian IT services company HCLT, unabashedly prioritizes employees and organizational structure over customers. In *Employees First, Customers Second*, Nayar credits the empowerment of *value zone* employees (those in contact with customers) as a key competitive strength. He also lauds a culture of introspection, change, and transparency for helping his organization stay focused on the right things. Tactics used by HCLT include 360-degree employee reviews—largely removed from HR—as well as "employee first councils." These councils resemble college clubs and help decentralize the firm. Nayar credits the councils with increasing employee passion and improving the corporate culture.[45]

Laszlo Bock, Google's head of People Operations (Google speak for HR), describes the firm's HR function enthusiastically with, "More than anything, what unites us in People Operations is a vision that work doesn't need to be miserable. That it can be ennobling and energizing and exciting. This is what drives us."[46]

In his book *Work Rules!*, Bock conveys an infectious enthusiasm for the HR function, yet he is also pragmatic. Bock laments traditional, status quo compensation schemes and their attempts at fairness by declaring, "Most companies design compensation systems that encourage the best performers and those with the most potential to quit." He adds, "Pay unfairly: your best people are better than you think."[47] Indeed, top performers and rising stars at many companies are grossly underpaid and likely serving on too many projects. Visibility and challenging assignments may motivate these stars in the short run, but eventually resentment and burnout seep in.

Let's be clear, Google can well afford to be progressive in its HR thinking thanks to their success and enormous resources. In contrast, the HR function at non-elite firms is often ignored and under-resourced. I joke that many HR departments are neither human nor resourceful, but this is very often the case. Scores of HR functions have been outsourced by companies over the last several years with no sign of the trend abating. Many upper management teams view HR simply as a support function that costs the firm money.

The Academic-Practitioner Divide on Human Resources

Scholars have not ignored the plight of *les miserables* on the job. However, the academy has not been able to galvanize much reaction from within its own ranks nor has it truly connected with the larger body of management practitioners that it hopes to enlighten.

The party line among academics that examine the impact of HR practices on organizations is that these practices, in general, have a positive effect on their respective firms. OK, this makes sense. The better the firm is at recruiting, training, providing benefits, formally appraising performance, and giving regular raises, then the better the firm is likely to perform financially and be viewed positively by employees. However, a conundrum exists concerning reverse causality and causal order. Is the firm performing well because it has wonderful HR management practices, or are HR practices more robust because the company has been performing well financially? Which came first, the chicken or the egg? While many techniques have been used to test for reverse causality, this remains a problematic issue in management research.[48]

A longitudinal study of 336 small to medium-sized enterprises (SMEs) in the United Kingdom concluded that HR practices "positively enhanced sustained competitive advantage."[49] Sounds impressive. However, the study, published in the *International Small Business Journal*, used a subjective indicator for this so-called *sustained competitive advantage*. Hard numbers on financial performance were not forthcoming from respondents. While a sustained competitive advantage is a rare breed and likely not a reality for most of these SMEs, the study did show a positive relationship between HR practices and perceived firm performance relative to competitors.

Another study reviewed nearly 250 research papers focused on either HR *management* or HR *development*, and their relationship to organizational performance. The study, appearing in *Human Resource Development Review*, emphasized the similarities and complementary nature of the two HR perspectives. Furthermore, the author unscientifically opined that HR was "the most important of all organizational resources."[50] This claim was not substantiated in the paper. The study emphasized the need for more scholars to study linkages between HR and organizational performance, as well as the importance of the HR function to have a strategic voice in the firm. Lastly, the author hoped the two HR disciplines (i.e., management and development) "would help in fully translating the 'people are our most valuable assets' rhetoric into reality."[51] As a responsible behavioral scientist, the study author appears unconvinced for now, and rightfully so.

A 2015 *Harvard Business Review* issue contained several informative articles on the importance of the HR function. One article, boldly titled "People Before Strategy," captured the essence of HR's need to become more relevant, stating:

> In keeping with recasting HR as a value creator rather than a cost center, performance should be measured by outputs that are more closely linked to revenue, profit margin, brand recognition, or market share. And the closer the linkage, the better.[52]

OK, aside from measuring sales representative productivity, the above prescription is nearly impossible to fulfill. This same article went on to suggest that predictive analytics serve as a value adder for HR—an excellent suggestion showing HR is hip and data driven. The article also proposed comparing the role of the Chief HR Officer to the Chief Financial Officer (CFO). This raises an interesting question: Why is it that Finance, essentially a support function in most firms (like HR), does not get the same evil-eye scrutiny and "scraps from the table" treatment that has befallen HR? Senior management apparently sees more value in staff that presides over cash, debt, and income statements versus personnel and systems responsible for cultivating human capital. Does that seem sensible? Aren't both important?

Forbes reported in 2015 that only 14 percent of surveyed companies had analytics capabilities for HR. *Forbes* also claimed that just "fifteen percent of senior business leaders say they changed a business decision in response to an HR insight in the past year."[53]

Consulting firm Deloitte surveys employees and leaders throughout the world regarding human capital. In 2014, Deloitte reported that "sixty-five percent of executives in our survey rated 'overwhelmed employee' an 'urgent' or 'important trend;' while forty-four percent said that they are 'not ready' to deal with it." Deloitte's recommendation to alleviate the overwhelmed is to simplify the work of these employees.[54] Good suggestion. However, nearly half the managers queried are too overwhelmed themselves to help the overwhelmed. Fifty-seven percent of nearly 500 HR executives rated their capability as "weak" in terms of "helping employees manage information and schedules."[55] Again, firms are doing a good job of listening to employees and sensing their collective angst, but the fundamental problem is a lack of mobilized resources to help the besieged masses.

In their comprehensive *Global Human Capital Trends 2016* report, Deloitte cited improvements in the HR function worldwide, but commented that just 1 year earlier HR was in need of an "extreme makeover." Deloitte went further with, "HR skills were weak, companies were not spending enough on developing HR professionals, and HR itself was too focused on service delivery and not enough on building consulting skills."[56] Ouch! Shame on all those HR do-gooders trying to deliver services to their employees in need.

I believe the majority of senior managers would like to help alleviate the plight of their downtrodden employees. Unfortunately, the added cost of doing so and the financial metrics of short-time horizons dissuade management from increasing funding for actionable HR intervention. Conventional fiscal prudence dictates that more HR functions will likely be outsourced. And perhaps specialized HR firms are better equipped to deal with the complexities of human assets. However, the general management ranks seem unconvinced that increases in HR spending will result in improved organizational performance.

Even in its disadvantaged state, the HR function has lots of talented, dedicated professionals. If given the chance, they could bolster the human condition of their HR (i.e., the select superstars *and* everyone else). Organizations should adopt best-in-class HR practices where it matters strategically. Senior management should invest wisely in people—at least until the robots come for them, too.

Contra Maxims for People as Assets

A select few of our people may be our most important assets. Involve and engage your employee assets. Ask your employees how to improve business performance. *Every* employee needs a compelling value proposition. Most employees are not as vital as the business models that they serve.

Notes

1. Charles Handy, *The Empty Raincoat: Making Sense of the Future* (London, United Kingdom: Hutchinson, 1994), 23.
2. Passard Dean, Kaitlin McKenna and Vyas Krishnan, "Accounting for Human Capital: Is the Balance Sheet Missing Something," *International Journal of Business & Social Science* 3, no. 12 (2012): 61–64. For a helpful explanation of problems with quantifying human capital, see Andrew Mayo, "Financial Statements and Human Capital," *Management Extra,* June 2008. Middlesex Business School. http://www.mayolearning.com/assets/Uploads/Publications/ICAEWMay-08-Measuring-Human-Capital.pdf For an academic economist's valuation method, see Andrea Eisfeldt and Dimitris Papanikolaou, "The Value and Ownership of Intangible Capital," *American Economic Review: Papers and Proceedings* 104, no. 5 (2014): 189–194. http://doi.org/10.1257/aer.104.5.189

3. Jeffrey Pfeffer and Robert Sutton, *Hard Facts, Dangerous Half-truths & Total Nonsense* (Boston, MA: Harvard Business School Press, 2006), 96.

4. Gary Hamel, *The Future of Management* (Boston, MA: Harvard Business School Press, 2007), 130.

5. Karen Vaugh, "John Locke and the Labor Theory of Value," *Journal of Libertarian Studies* 2, no. 4 (1978): 311–326. Cited from Peter Laslett (Ed.), *Locke's Two Treatises of Civil Government, 2nd ed.* (Cambridge, MA: Cambridge University Press, 1967), 313.

6. Annamarie Mann and Jim Harter, "The Worldwide Employee Engagement Crisis," 7 Jan 2016, http://www.gallup.com/businessjournal/188033/worldwide-employee-engagement-crisis.aspx (accessed Feb 23, 2016).

7. Ibid.

8. The Conference Board, *Staying Ahead of Change and Preparing for 2020: Insights from the 2015 Corporate Brand and Reputation Conference*, 6 Nov 2015, https://www.conference-board.org/pdfdownload.cfm?masterProductID=9998 (accessed Mar 29, 2016).

9. Josh Bersin, Dimple Agarwal, Bill Pelster and Jeff Schwartz (Eds.), *Global Human Capital Trends 2015: Leading in the New World of Work* (Deloitte University Press, 2015), 36, http://d27n205l7rookf.cloudfront.net/wp-content/uploads/2015/08/DUP_GlobalHumanCapitalTrends2015.pdf

10. *The Economist*, "The Enemy Within," 25 July 2015, 53.

11. Bill Pelster and Jeff Schwartz (Eds.), *Global Human Capital Trends 2016: The New Organization: Different by Design* (Deloitte University Press, 2016). http://www2.deloitte.com/global/en/pages/human-capital/articles/introduction-human-capital-trends.html (accessed Mar 10, 2016).

12. Society for Human Resource Management, *2015 Employee Job Satisfaction and Engagement* (Alexandria, VA: SHRM, 2015), https://www.shrm.org/Research/SurveyFindings/Documents/2015-Job-Satisfaction-and-Engagement-Report.pdf (accessed Mar 24, 2016). SHRM note on engagement: The 2015 SHRM Report also surveyed for employee engagement aspects, but utilized a different scale and format than the Gallup poll discussed in the chapter. The SHRM Report indicated employees were "moderately engaged"—a much more positive

finding than the Gallup results. This may be attributed to differences in methodology and the definition used for the engagement construct.

13. *Chicago Tribune*, "Poll Shows 3 in 4 at Work are Stressed," 26 Aug 2012, http://articles.chicagotribune.com/2012-08-26/business/ct-biz-0827-workplace-stress-20120827_1_workplace-stress-annoying-co-workers-everest-college (accessed Mar 24, 2016).

14. Carol Matlack and Giovanni Salzano, "Discouraged Workers Dog Europe's Recovery," *Bloomberg Businessweek*, Mar 21–27, 2016, 16–18.

15. Handy, *Empty Raincoat*, 26.

16. Bureau of Labor Statistics (2016). Real Earnings – January 2016. Retrieved 2 Mar 2016 from http://www.bls.gov/news.release/pdf/realer.pdf

17. Stephen Greenhouse, "The Mystery of the Vanishing Pay Raise," *The New York Times*, 1 Nov 2015, SR3.

18. Steven Greenhouse, *The Big Squeeze: Tough Times for the American Worker* (New York, NY: Knopf, 2008).

19. Chad Syverson, *Challenges to Mismeasurement Explanations for the U.S. Productivity Slowdown, Working Paper* (Cambridge, MA: National Bureau of Economic Research, 2016), http://www.nber.org/papers/w21974 (accessed Mar 6, 2016).

20. Tyler Cowen, "A Slowdown that Silicon Valley Doesn't Believe," *The New York Times*, 6 Mar 2016, BU6.

21. The Conference Board, *Prioritizing Productivity to Drive Growth, Competitiveness, and Profitability. Strategic Overview*, June 2015, https://www.conference-board.org/pdfdownload.cfm?masterProductID=9644 (accessed Mar 28, 2016).

22. Jodi Kantor and David Streitfeld, "Amazon's Bruising, Thrilling Workplace," *New York Times*, 16 Aug 2015, 20–22.

23. Upton Sinclair, *The Jungle* (New York, NY: Barnes & Noble Books, 2003) [originally published in 1906].

24. Ryan Mac, "Jeff Bezos Calls Amazon 'Best Place in the World to Fail' in Shareholder Letter," *Forbes*, 5 Apr 2016, http://www.forbes.com/sites/ryanmac/2016/04/05/jeff-bezos-calls-amazon-best-place-in-the-world-to-fail-in-shareholder-letter/#4eda899c62f4 (accessed Apr 6, 2016).

25. Jim Collins, *Good to Great: Why Some Companies Make the Leap ... and Others Don't* (New York, NY: Harper Business, 2001), 51.

26. *The Economist*, "Digital Taylorism: A Modern Version of 'Scientific Management' Threatens to Dehumanize the Workplace," 12 Sep 2015, 63.

27. Esther Kaplan, "The Spy Who Fired Me: The Human Costs of Workplace Monitoring," *Harper's*, Mar 2015, 31–40.

28. Ibid.

29. Lamar Pierce, Daniel Snow and Andrew McAffee, "Cleaning House: The Impact of Information Technology Monitoring on Employee Theft and Productivity," *Management Science*, May 2015, DOI: 10.2139/ssrn.2318592

30. Aaron De Smet, Susan Lund and Robert Schaninger, "Organizing for the Future," *McKinsey Quarterly*, Jan 2016, http://www.mckinsey .com/business-functions/organization/our-insights/organizing-for-the-future?cid=other-eml-ttn-mip-mck-oth-1604 (accessed Apr 4, 2016).

31. Pew Research Center, *AI, Robots, and the Future of Jobs,* Aug 2014, http://www.pewinternet.org/files/2014/08/Future-of-AI-Robotics-and-Jobs.pdf

32. Carl Frey and Michael Osborne, *The Future of Employment: How Susceptible are Jobs to Computerization?* 17 Sep 2013, 38, http:// www.oxfordmartin.ox.ac.uk/downloads/academic/The_Future_of_ Employment.pdf

33. Erik Brynjolfsson and Andrew McAfee, *The Second Machine Age: Work, Progress, and Prosperity in a Time of Brilliant Technologies* (New York, NY: W.W. Norton, 2014), 11.

34. TD Ameritrade. Advertisement in *The Atlantic* (April, 2016), 20. Advertisement for Amerivest Managed Portfolios. Full page ad depicts baby boomer-types doing awkward robot dance moves. Copy heading reads: "Outsourcing more robot jobs to humans." Body copy includes ". . . . if you ever need a *little* [italics mine] assistance, our experienced service team is available to discuss your portfolio. Because let's face it, no one wants to talk with a robot." Advertisement is touting the automated, rule-based criteria of the portfolio while human interaction is permitted (but only *a little bit*).

35. Nathaniel Popper, "Stocks & Bots," *The New York Times Magazine*, 28 Feb 2016, 56–62, 71.

36. Spencer Soper, "The Robots Chasing Amazon," *Bloomberg Businessweek*, 26 Oct–1 Nov, 2015, 30–31.

37. Ibid.

38. Bill Bremner, Isabel Reynolds, Ting Shi and Rose Kim, "Japan Unleashes a Robot Revolution," *Bloomberg Businessweek*, 1–7 Jun 2015, 16–18.

39. Brynjolfsson and McAfee, *Second Machine Age* (New York, NY: W.W. Norton & Company, 2014), 246–247.

40. Anna Coote, Jane Franklin and Andrew Simms, *21 Hours: Why a Shorter Working Week Can Help Us All to Flourish in the 21st Century* (London, United Kingdom: New Economics Foundation, 2010).

41. *The Economist*, "France's Labour Reforms: Working Nine to Four," 5 Mar 2016, 48–49.

42. Ibid.

43. Hamel, *Future of Management*.

44. John Kell, "Dancing in the Aisles," *Fortune: Investor's Guide 2016*, 15 Dec 2015, 26.

45. Vineet Nayar, *Employees First, Customers Second* (Boston, MA: Harvard Business Press, 2010).

46. Laszlo Bock, *Work rules!: Insights From Inside Google That Will Transform How You Live and Lead* (New York, NY: Twelve, 2015), 234.

47. Ibid.

48. Gerhard Kling, Charles Harvey and Mairi MacLean, "Establishing Causal Order in Longitudinal Studies Combining Binary and Continuous Dependent Variables," *Organizational Research Methods*, (2015): 1–30. DOI: 10.1177/1094428115618760

49. Maura Sheehan, "Human Resource Management and Performance: Evidence from Small and Medium-sized Firms," *International Small Business Journal* 32, no. 5 (2014): 545–570.

50. Meera Alagaraja, "HRD and HRM Perspectives on Organizational Performance: A Review of Literature," *Human Resource Development Review* 12, no. 2 (2012): 117–143.

51. Ibid.

52. Ram Charan, Dominic Barton and Dennis Carey, "People Before Strategy: A New Role for the CHRO," *Harvard Business Review*, July–August 2015, 8.
53. *Forbes*, "The HR Guide to the Galaxy," 25 May 2015, 90–91.
54. Tom Hodson, Jeff Schwartz, Ardie van Berkel and Ian Winston Otten, *The Overwhelmed Employee: Simplify the Work Environment* (Deloitte University Press, Mar 7, 2014), http://dupress.com/articles/hc-trends-2014-overwhelmed-employee/ (accessed Mar 15, 2016).
55. Ibid.
56. Pelster and Schwartz (Eds.) *Global Human Capital Trends 2016*.

CHAPTER 4

Diversity Improves Performance

Diversity is less a function of the isolation of groups than of the relationships which unite them.

—Claude Levi-Strauss, *Structural Anthropology, Vol 2*

The key word among advocates of multiculturalism became "diversity." Sweeping claims for the benefits of demographic and cultural diversity in innumerable institutions and circumstances have prevailed without a speck of evidence being asked for or given. It is one of the purest examples of arguments without arguments, and of the force of sheer repetition, insistence and intimidation.

—Thomas Sowell, *Intellectuals and Race*

A cultural third rail, diversity is seldom discussed in rational, evidence-based tones. The virtues of la différence can be real or mythological depending on the context. Diversity evokes a range of emotions, arguments, theories, biases, and rhetoric. This chapter makes no claim of completely taming the hydra that is the diversity debate. The objective here is far simpler: to call attention to thoughtful opinion and empirical evidence that counter the absoluteness of the maxim *Diversity improves performance*. Diversity may be beneficial in many instances, but it is far from a guarantee of better outcomes.

I'll present a dispassionate review of diversity as an explanatory variable with regard to the performance of firms, work teams, senior management, and boards of directors. I'll also provide a brief look at how diversity is treated at U.S. universities. A thoughtful dialogue on diversity can be difficult for many, even when confronted with compelling evidence.

Recall in the introductory chapter brief mentions of the largely homogenous institutions of the nursing profession, the National Basketball Association (NBA), the venture capital industry, and Silicon Valley senior executives. Nursing is overwhelmingly female (90.4 percent) and highly regarded as a profession for providing health care at all levels of the care continuum.[1] For the NBA, most of the players are long (average height is 6 ft 7 in) and all are athletic.[2] Even with increasing numbers of European players, roughly three-quarters of NBA players are black.[3] The NBA is indisputably the best basketball league in the world. Note that there are very few pro-diversity calls to make the nursing profession more male, or the NBA shorter and less black. Nor should there be.

Silicon Valley is responsible for creating the modern venture capital industry, the microprocessor, and world-beating tech firms such as Apple, Google, Intel, PayPal, and Hewlett-Packard. Largely comprised of white males, the leadership ranks of Silicon Valley's start-up and corporate community are envied by much of the world. However, when *The Atlantic* conducted their annual Silicon Valley Insiders Poll in 2015, 63 percent of respondents rated the severity of sexism in tech at seven or above (on a scale of one to ten, with ten being the most severe) and 68 percent scored the seriousness of a lack of ethnic and racial diversity in tech with the same rating.[4]

A recent article in the Wharton School's online journal claimed, "U.S. corporations spend $8 billion annually on diversity training. Yet a meta-review of almost a thousand studies finds a 'dearth of evidence' about their efficacy."[5] Such data and interpretations should compel us to ask more questions about widespread business practices and beliefs about diversity. And so that is what we shall do.

Goodness of Fit

Researchers often refer to a *goodness of fit* test when appraising the predictive value of a statistical model. Like the fit of your favorite pair of jeans, an organization desires a nice fit among its members and internal culture.

Fit has also become a way to describe a new hire (e.g., "He's a good fit for the team," or "She'll fit right in here at headquarters") as well as communicating termination: "We have to let you go because this really isn't a good fit, nothing against you personally." Homogeneity in the workplace is often explained by a model called the Similarity/Attraction Paradigm. The model theorizes that people feel more comfortable being around others that are much like themselves. Positive reinforcement is more likely to occur thanks to similar cultural backgrounds.[6]

A lack of fit is often the reason diverse members of a group feel uncomfortable or stressed, and this contributes to high turnover rates.[7] You may hear some disaffected employee say, "This place just doesn't get me." This may be true, but it is the responsibility of both the employee and the employer to make things work. This applies to schools and other communities as well. If you are a new employee, student, or citizen, you have to *get them* in terms of the culture of which you are a part. Too often, we place the burden only on the workplace, school, or greater culture for making sure the larger entity *gets* the new member. It is not easy to be new in a strange environment. It is often harder for those who are new *and* different. The difference may include one or more of the following characteristics: race, ethnicity, age, gender, tenure, sociocultural or socioeconomic background, level and type of education, physical appearance, physical or intellectual ability, personality type, preferred language, national origin, geography, customs, values, spirituality, sexuality, political ideology, approaches to problems, functional skill set, level of team orientation, leisure activities, type of dress, and even diet preferences. Regardless of what makes someone different, fitting in is a shared responsibility. Two-way empathy matters.

Globalization's Messy Role

In the interest of full disclosure, I am a globalist and free and fair trade advocate. I am an enthusiastic proponent of cross-cultural exchange, be it through trade, art, education, travel, or media. Most of us are aware of the disruptions caused by globalization, especially in the near term. However, we are products of different cultures due to past interactions with dissimilar people and customs. Globalization, while imperfect, will continue to get more people out of extreme poverty than any global policy initiative in the foreseeable future.

Tyler Cowen, an economics professor at George Mason University, sheds light on a diversity paradox that has resulted from globalization. Simply put, diversity *within* cultures rises as a result of cross-cultural exchanges. Paradoxically, diversity and differences *across* cultures decrease. For example, the United States grows more diverse due to immigration, trade, and other forms of exchange. The countries on the other side of these exchanges become less unique in their own right and become more like the United States, even if only in small ways initially.[8]

Look at the many shared characteristics between Canada, the United States, and Mexico. Increased trade, travel, and cross border consumption of media and entertainment have made the three countries more similar to each other and less unique from the perspective of outsiders. As Mexicans settle and have children in the United States, they make the United States a little more Mexican. As U.S. companies build cars in Mexico, they make Mexico a little less Mexican (i.e., in an arbitrary, historical sense) and a bit more American (whatever that means).

Results of globalization can be far reaching, unpredictable, and occasionally tragic. As economist and author Thomas Sowell reminds us, "Napoleon was not French, Stalin was not Russian, and Hitler was not German."[9] Today, Europe grapples with a sizable influx of immigrants. Even before the recent diaspora out of the Middle East, there has been a rising backlash against multiculturalism throughout much of Europe over the last several years.[10]

Many so-called advocates of diversity are conflicted when diversity erodes local specialness or creates imbalances. Cowen, in *Creative Destruction: How Globalization is Changing the World's Cultures*, points to the concentrated power and global distribution clout of the U.S. film industry as an example. Those bemoaning U.S. movie dominance long for films from other countries. Interestingly, film makers outside the United States are more diverse because of influences from American cinema just as American directors are enriched by techniques from foreign film makers.

Cowen calls out those who are inconsistent with their conditional demands for diversity, accusing them of having *particularist agendas*. He illustrates this with the distinction between "diversity at any single point in time and *diversity across time.*" For instance, should a culture that is losing its traditional trappings be allowed to morph on its own? Does anyone have the right to "freeze cultures in a specialized era" because that is how certain observers frame that culture? Where does this selective preservation cross the line and wrongfully inhibit younger generations or others seeking change from outside influences?[11] Counterintuitively, Cowen offers, "Most generally, partial homogenization often creates the conditions necessary for diversity to flower on the micro level."[12] Globalization does indeed enable change, cultural dynamism, and yes—diversity!

A recent report by global consulting giant McKinsey & Company is indicative of the common diversity narrative in business today. McKinsey's 2015 *Diversity Matters* project combed data from 366 public companies in the United States, Canada, Latin America, and the United Kingdom. The final report reveals just 16 percent of executive team members in the United States are women, and females make up only 12 percent of executives in the United Kingdom and 6 percent in Brazil.[13]

McKinsey's report claims that companies in the top quartile for gender diversity are "15% more likely to have financial returns above their respective national industry medians." For racial and ethnic diversity, those firms in the top quartile are 35 percent more likely to exceed industry performance medians.[14] The report cautions that these figures are correlations and do not represent causal links. However, the language in the report repeatedly implies a direct linkage. For example, the executive summary of the report states:

> The findings nonetheless permit reasonable hypotheses on what is driving improved performance by companies with diverse executive teams and boards. It stands to reason—and has been demonstrated in other studies, as we indicate—that more diverse companies are better able to win top talent, and improve their customer orientation, employee satisfaction, and decision making and innovation, leading to a virtuous cycle of increasing returns.[15]

McKinsey should spare the reader from this biased conjuring of dividends "demonstrated in other studies." The report's warnings about the erroneous interpretation of statistics are followed up by their own erroneous interpretation of statistics. Unfortunately, the report contains no discussion on the likelihood of reverse causality or halo effects. The report does, however, reveal how companies can become more diverse. After all, diversity is big business and you can't be expected to enrich your firm's diversity on your own. Fear not, McKinsey & Company (along with other capable consulting firms) is here to help. Thankfully, the overt pitch for McKinsey's diversity consulting services is left out of the *Diversity Matters* report.

A Matter of Perspective

Scott Page, University of Michigan professor of complex systems, political science, and economics, provides a useful framework for seeing the value of *relevant* diversity. Page distinguishes between identity-based categorizations (e.g., race, ethnicity, gender, and age) by emphasizing cognitively based differences in individuals. Page's *Diversity Trumps Ability Theorem* attempts to model the conditions necessary for a group of diverse (and knowledgeable) individuals to be more effective than an expert or group of like-minded experts. For instance, a group of specialized rocket scientists may get stuck on a problem largely because they share the same perspective or approach to solving it. They have similar backgrounds and training. Bringing in outside consultants, who are not necessarily smarter but possess alternative perspectives, will likely produce more novel solutions. Page refers to this synergistic effect from varying viewpoints as *superadditivity*.[16]

In order for diversity to outperform ability in a problem-solving context, Page stresses that the following conditions should be present: (a) the problem is hard (otherwise a lone expert would have a higher success rate); (b) the people involved are smart (acceptable degree of content knowledge); (c) the contributors are diverse (different backgrounds and perspectives); and (d) the teams are large enough and chosen from a sizable pool.[17]

Page also devised a *Diversity Prediction Theorem* that derives value from a diverse set of interpretations when tackling a predictive scenario. Forecasting product sales is a good example. Results from forecasting are very often wrong even when performed by the best marketing prognosticator in a company. This expert is likely relying on her favorite forecast method, a tool she knows well and has used in the past. However, if you combine the interpretations and predictive models from a group of diverse professionals (e.g., sales representatives, distributors, service personnel, product managers, ad agency contacts, and consumer behavior consultants), you will likely end up with a more accurate forecast than the one proposed by the so-called expert. Page's logic may be summed up with the following:

> Rather than having a single perspective, interpretation, heuristic, or predictive model, people and organizations should have many. We must become Whitmanesque and contain multitudes. The advantages of containing multitudes should be clear. Diverse perspectives and heuristics improve problem solving. Diverse interpretations and predictive models lead to more accurate predictions. Crowds are not wise, but crowds of models are.[18]

In his 2007 book *The Difference: How the Power of Diversity Creates Better Groups, Firms, Schools, and Societies,* Page provides a compelling case for the benefits of properly grouped, diverse thinking. He does, however, point to high correlations of identity characteristics with cognitive similarities. Unfortunately, the often stipulated diversity defaults are race, ethnicity, or gender. Lost is an opportunity to exploit the rich differences of many other diversity characteristics.

Highly related to diversity of perspective is diversity of thought. Amit Singh, President of Google for Work, recently said in a *New York Times* interview that "Diversity of thought is actually the most invaluable thing in a business community. If we're always agreeing with each other, then we haven't gone down paths of debate that allow new ideas to emerge."[19]

During a Bloomberg Television program marking the commemoration of International Women's Day in March 2016, General Electric's Vice Chair Beth Comstock was asked repeatedly about gender disparities on corporate boards. Comstock responded, "We should have more women in key leadership positions. . . . I'm a big believer that diversity equals innovation.... Innovation comes from diversity of thought. . . . You want more diverse perspectives, more diverse experiences." Comstock went on to stress the importance of hiring the right individuals, and sometimes you should work hard to hire people that are different from yourself.[20]

One of the more constructive accounts of diversity in business comes from Martin Davidson of the University of Virginia's Darden School. In *The End of Diversity as We Know It*, Davidson proposes the adoption of a broader set of diversity criteria, going well beyond traditional, salient characteristics. He recommends that businesses actively leverage the differences among employees. While he acknowledges the "unqualified assertion that any kind of diversity will lead to superior performance is just wrong," he stresses that there is hope for diversity efforts. Davidson cites strategic linkages, recognition and appraisal of differences (even nuanced), transparency, and inclusivity as keys to exploiting the "dynamics of differences."[21]

A Diverse Look at Diversity Research

Given the massive amounts of research completed to date on diversity in organizations, a complete account of those findings is not feasible. However, I provide a concise and representative review of empirical scholarship and relevant commentary from this domain. I include a few studies conducted as meta-analyses for reasons of economy and comprehensiveness.

I begin with a five-year field study exploring the relationships between gender and racial diversity and business performance. The work was completed by a team of nine scholars from several prominent research universities, forming a group called the Diversity Research Network. The team studied four large (all Fortune 500) companies from an initial list of 20 firms that expressed interest in enhancing diversity management programs. Thus, there is a distinct possibility of self-selection bias with this diversity-attuned cohort of firms.

Results indicated "few direct effects of diversity on performance—either positive or negative."[22] Additionally, a negative effect of racial diversity on performance was amplified in situations with high competitiveness among teams. One firm exhibited a positive relationship between gender diversity and group processes, but racial diversity had the opposite effect. In the case of a large retailer, "Communities with more Whites, Blacks, Hispanics, or Asians did not buy more from stores with similar employees."[23] Findings from a financial services company showed racially diverse branches had a positive influence on overall performance, but only in the context of there being robust "integration-and-learning" programs present at those branch locations. In other words, diversity has a better chance of mattering (positively) if that diversity is leveraged with educational programs, training, and development regarding diversity issues.

The authors summarized the *Report of the Diversity Network* by saying, "The simplistic business case of the past [for diversity] is simply not supported." They recommend a reframing of the business case for diversity by urging diversity professionals, industry leaders, and scholars to "recognize that while there is no reason to believe diversity will naturally translate into better or worse results, diversity is both a labor-market imperative and societal expectation and value."[24] The report stressed the use of more sophisticated data analysis with regard to diversity efforts, as well as more experimentation in the field. While field work is more cumbersome to conduct, members of the Diversity Research Network feel the artificiality of laboratory settings may overstate observed effects of diversity.[25]

In a meta-analysis of empirical studies examining workforce diversity and organizational performance published in *Human Resource Management*, Michele Jayne of Ford Motor Company and Robert Dipboye of the University of Central Florida acknowledged problems with diversity rhetoric, expectations, and goal orientation of many corporate diversity programs. Key interpretations from this duo's review included (1) Increased demographic diversity "does not guarantee an increase in diversity of task-related knowledge, skills, abilities, experiences or other characteristics;" (2) "Increased diversity does not necessarily build commitment, improve motivation, and reduce conflict;" (3) Increases in group level diversity do not consistently lead to improved group performance and may introduce additional conflicts; and (4) Although results are mixed, increased diversity does not necessarily lead to improved organizational performance.[26]

To improve outcomes from diversity initiatives, Jayne and Dipboye recommend the following: use clear goals and metrics; tailor programs to context-specific needs; obtain buy-in across all levels of the organizations (especially upper management); emphasize the team-building process; and link diversity outcomes to the firm's strategy and business results.[27]

Another study, hypothesizing a positive performance impact from women in senior management positions, looked at S&P 1500 firms over a span of 15 years. The results were published in a 2012 issue of the *Strategic Management Journal* and used a reliable data set. The researchers concluded that their hypothesis was supported "only to the extent that a firm's strategy is focused on innovation, in which context the informational and societal benefits of gender diversity and the behaviors with women in management are likely to be especially important for managerial task performance."[28] Say what now? That sounds like a conclusion desperate to show a positive linkage with females in senior management. This paper claimed to test its results for reverse causality (i.e., checking if female executives were added *after* firms became contextually successful) and rationalized that positive results may be due to the "human capital advantages" of female executives.[29] Unfortunately, these conclusions overreach with wishful interpretations that are becoming more common in this research domain.

In 2016, Harvard behavioral economist and professor Iris Bohnet released *What Works: Gender Equality by Design*. Bohnet cited research that stressed the importance of role models as a key contributor to making professional careers more gender balanced. She also demonstrated how the method used to select diverse teams is critical in order to minimize unintentional gender biases. Bohnet also cautioned that "In short, diversity can lead to better performance—but not always."[30]

A paper in the *Academy of Management Journal*, looking at the effect of racial diversity on performance at over 500 banks, produced statistical models yielding negative and neutral results. The author concludes that racial diversity added value "within the proper context." This context consisted of banks undergoing a growth strategy, meaning they were performing well in terms of financial and market metrics. The paper cited costs associated with diversity efforts may be problematic in cases where a downsizing strategy is in effect. To the researcher's credit, he did surmise that some high-profit banks may have added diversity efforts *after* strong financial results (i.e., reverse causality) rather than the other way around.[31]

Diversity and Teamwork: Context is King

The adoption of cross-functional teams in the workplace is arguably one of the most widespread applications of diversity in the history of business. Prior to recent trends of telecommuting and the virtualization of geographically dispersed teams, the matrix organization grew to dominate the organization of work in many companies. The primary offspring of the matrix organization is the cross-functional team. How else could we get marketing to communicate with R&D, and R&D to play nice with manufacturing, and for anyone to sit and talk with cost accounting? Seriously though, cross-fertilization of functional skill sets can be both advantageous and disruptive to group processes and outcomes.

A football team is a good example of diverse skill sets coming together to accomplish shared goals. Teams have specialized individuals that strategize, coach, throw, catch, kick, run fast, block, and tackle. Cross-functional teams are similar in scope to football squads. There has been a great deal of research done trying to determine what makes a successful high-performing team. The last few decades have produced mixed results regarding the influence of demographic and task-oriented diversity on team outcomes.

A meta-analysis, reviewing 35 studies and reported in the *Journal of Management*, revealed support for the positive influence of task-related diversity on team performance. However, this study found bio-demographic diversity did not significantly relate to team performance, nor did diversity affect social integration (i.e., member satisfaction and team cohesion). Researchers recommended that organizations should "consciously create a high-performing team with members reflecting more task-relevant heterogeneity while focusing less on bio-demographic attributes."[32] The paper also concluded that organizational context may have a large impact on social integration. For example, team training programs and the level of leadership commitment can impact how group members interact and thus perform.

Another meta-study, published in the *Journal of Product Innovation Management*, focused on 38 studies to determine what makes new product development (NPD) teams more successful. Researchers found group cohesiveness to be a positive indicator of NPD performance (i.e., the more cohesive the team, the better the performance). Note the extant research usually posits team cohesiveness as important to team processes, with diversity having a disruptive effect on cohesiveness. Interestingly, this meta-analysis found no positive impact of functional diversity on team performance. The double-edged sword of functional diversity may spark creativity and improve problem solving in one setting, while foster-ing "emotional conflict" in another.[33]

The paradoxical nature of diversity in the workplace appears hinged on the resources put in place to encourage the leveraging of differences. This cognitive resource perspective involves promoting an "affirming cli-mate of diversity."[34] This obviously comes with a cost. Contrastingly, or-ganizations less apt to engage in diversity-related support programs run the risk of disruption and reduced performance from a diverse workforce.

As we'll see next with a review of boardroom diversity, gender has been a popular diversity variable for management scholars. Prior to 2000, gender studies within the suite of Academy of Management publications outnumbered race-related papers by a factor of three-to-two. Since 2000, management scholarship studying gender has outnumbered race-focused works by a five-to-one ratio.[35] This reductionist approach to diversity (in terms of scholarly focus) favors gender at the expense of race and other diversity indicators. This trend mirrors a past criticism of the feminist movement which asserted that women of color were not welcome in the broader feminist tent, resulting in black women missing out on subse-quent feminist advances in the latter part of the 20th century.[36]

Boardroom Bros

The corporate board of directors, as an institution, has received an enor-mous amount of scrutiny and scholarly attention over the last few de-cades. The relatively low incidence of female corporate directors has been a popular research theme.

For the Conference Board, Stanford's Deborah Rhode and Amanda Packel recounted their findings and interpretations regarding diversity on corporate boards from a 2014 article in *The Delaware Journal of Corporate Law*. Citing data from the Spencer Stuart U.S. Board Index 2014, women account for 19 percent of S&P 500 board seats, and just 13 percent of those in Russell 3000 firms.[37] The authors acknowledged there is much to be done to attain "more equitable leadership structures."[38] Their sugges-tions included mandatory interviews of minorities for open board seats (in the spirit of the National Football League's [NFL's] "Rooney Rule"), maintaining female board seats for those presently female, and targets for minority representation in the near term. Incidentally, Scandinavian countries have markedly increased the ranks of female board members partly through the use of targets and legislated mandates.

Rhodes and Packel acknowledge that the traditional business case for board diversity offers inconsistent results, and therefore does not offer a convincing case to shareholders in terms of financial returns. Instead, they argue on the side of diversity initiatives for "reputational arguments" and societal equity.[39]

An ambitious meta-analysis consisting of 140 studies examined the relationship between women on boards and firms' financial performance. Published in a 2015 issue of the *Academy of Management Journal*, this paper suggested that "board diversity is neither wholly detrimental nor wholly beneficial to firm financial performance."[40] This paper noted that board independence (examined because female directors are more likely to be independent board members) does not materially influence a firm's performance. The study concluded that the level of female board representation is positively related to more diligent monitoring and strategy involvement by the board.[41] This finding is a common silver lining trumpeted by researchers desiring positive linkages from female board membership, at least when compared to boards with fewer or no females.

A report in 2012 received a great deal of media buzz when it touted that female executives give venture-backed start-ups a greater chance of succeeding. Published by Dow Jones, Inc., the *Women at the Wheel* report studied over 20,000 venture capital (VC)-backed firms from 1997 to 2011. The report claimed, "The overall median proportion of female executives is 7.1% at successful companies and 3.1% at unsuccessful companies [within the four largest industry sectors]."[42] Relying on some statistical gymnastics, the authors ventured further out on a limb as they, "claim with statistical significance that there is a dependence between a company having female executives and its success."[43] However, when looking at the entire data set (including more than just the top four sectors), the authors admit that "In the pool of successful companies versus failed companies, we do not see any significant difference between the proportion of female executives."[44]

A flaw with the initial claim above is that the report's definition of "unsuccessful companies" excludes several thousand firms characterized as "not yet successful." Additionally, the report acknowledges that women often join VC-backed firms later in their development (i.e., closer to being successful). This point is supported with the report's own finding that the incidence of female executives is "much higher" with VC-backed initial public offerings (IPOs) versus VC-backed firms that exit (as successes) via mergers and acquisitions.[45]

The media and the report's authors should share the blame for the misleading conclusions presented in the popular press about gender's fantastical impact on business performance.

Seemingly, in an effort to shame boards into becoming more diverse (in terms of females and minority representation), many researchers have attempted to show that female directors make for better performing companies. But doesn't this strike you as an odd proposition? Step back and ask yourself why would gender, or race, or ethnicity, or hair color matter significantly to the financial returns of a corporation? Why this obsession with finding the "El Dorado" of gender-based performance links? I maintain that these attributes should not matter, be it in the board room or C-level management ranks. The skills and behavior that get certain men to the top of corporations are fundamentally the same skills and behavior that benefit high-achieving women and minorities.

Recounting her study of over 900 top and middle managers in Norway (known for its progressive liberalism regarding gender and work), sociologist Anne Grethe Solberg concluded the following: "Leadership style can be independent from biological gender. Men and women don't have different styles of leadership. We should be cautious when working with gender balance and gender equality in organizations."[46]

Let's try a hypothetical. Suppose that all-female, all-black boards and black female CEOs are found to indicate superior financial results for their companies. If this were the case, I posit that 99 percent of the most bigoted investors would flock to invest in firms run by black females. Why? Because profits will trump sexist and racist ideology. Thomas Sowell once wrote, "Racists may prefer their own group to others, but they prefer themselves most of all."[47]

Centuries of past prejudice against women and minorities seem to have influenced the overstatement of benefits imagined from more proportional representation in upper management. Specious research conclusions and reckless public relations agendas are not uncommon. It is, to a large extent, irresponsibility from mostly good intentions. While scholars should be (and usually are) disinterested in their pursuit of truthful explanations, the lure of finding diversity linkages to performance may be too compelling for some. Frustration with the slow pace of change may have unfortunately created research streams that have drifted toward a more hopeful orientation, and away from a dispassionate approach required of social scientists.

Epicenters for Diversity Discourse

The forefront of the diversity debate is occurring where you might expect—U.S. colleges and universities. Idealism, young adulthood, intellectualism, a vibrant community of scholars, and (hopefully) the freedom to speak freely are hallmarks of a university campus. Diversity debates and controversies on campus often lead the country at large to further ruminate and discuss issues related to inequality, access, and policy.

Notable resistance to the swelling of college diversity initiatives came long ago from the likes of David Sacks and Peter Thiel. In their provocative book *The Diversity Myth: Multicultural and Political Intolerance on Campus*, the authors painstakingly describe the downside of political correctness and aggressive diversity efforts on college campuses. The book uses Stanford extensively as a case study, highlighting the overhaul of Stanford's curriculum and its loss of Western philosophy-oriented courses in exchange for more contemporary and diverse subjects.[48]

Sacks and Thiel point out the hypocrisy of many diversity initiatives that were created largely because of past intolerance. For example, themed dorms (e.g., ethnic or lifestyle-specific buildings) have been established as a way for certain minority students to feel more comfortable with their identities. Ironically, themed houses often represent a segregation redux. Sameness is purposefully clustered together, fostering a less integrated student body. Demands for *safe spaces* on campus and *trigger warnings* in classrooms are symptoms of hypersensitivity to potentially offensive language or exclusionary behavior.

The following captures the caution expressed in *The Diversity Myth*, and its challenge to wanton multiculturalism for its own sake:

> The new culture of multiculturalism (or "multiculture") defines its own taboos, creates its own mythos, initiates its own rites of passage, and distributes its own social roles. It is in many ways a self-contradictory culture—one that advocates liberation from moral certitude and all other forms of authority, but maintains itself with maximum authority and certainty of belief. This contradiction runs through the heart of the multiculture, and so runs through its denizens, whose daily choices ultimately must sustain it. Like all cultural systems, it has a sacred core—a bundle of values, superstitions, and beliefs never articulated by its citizens but fiercely guarded nonetheless. To pierce this sacred veil is to occasion sacrilege.[49]

Sacks and Thiel assail multicultural theology partly because of its attack on Western religion and its principles. As multiculturalism seeks to erode the *unfair* hegemony of Judeo-Christian values, the "new multicultural religion becomes transformed into a religion of antireligiosity."[50] Indeed, ideological conservatives have complained for years of the intolerance they encounter at universities and in the media.

Others warn that the revamping of college general education requirements, with rigid diversity components, acts as a platform for political thought reform. While rebuking recent strengthening of the diversity requirements at the University of Massachusetts Amherst, Daphne Patai and Harvey Silverglate (both board members of the Foundation for Individual Rights in Education, or FIRE) rouse with the following:

> In a society where students have long been granted the right to refuse, for example, to recite a biblical passage or even the Pledge of Allegiance in public schools, college students are now required to genuflect before the banner of diversity, inclusion and social justice. It's insufficient for students to refrain from uttering offensive or "wrong" words and ideas. They must increasingly be trained to mimic their professors and affirmatively utter the "right" ones.[51]

A major driver for diversity on campus is the admissions office. The diversity push by many universities runs the risk of creating diverse (in some ways) student populations comprised of nondiverse students (i.e., ultraspecialized individuals). Well-rounded students without distinct, unidimensional attributes are not what many elite institutions desire.

College admissions offices have long trumpeted the number of countries represented on campus. They enjoy touting that students from all 50 states make up the new class of freshman. Remarkably, many elite institutions proudly recount how each year they reject several students with perfect SAT scores. I know there are multiple forms of intelligence, but why would elite universities think rejecting academically gifted students (in favor of admitting students with dramatically lower scores) is a good idea? Does it help provide space for preferential groups, including underrepresented minorities, legacies, musicians, and athletes that may not qualify under normal admissions parameters?

Nearly 90 years ago Aldous Huxley wrote, in *Proper Studies*, "It is precisely for the philomaths that universities ought to cater."[52] Sadly, many universities have resorted to new ways of pursuing their research and education missions. Public relations-oriented diversity efforts and aggressive forays in the entertainment business (i.e., costly big-time athletics) have become commonplace in recent decades.

Forcing diversity breeds resentment and puts pressure and unwanted scrutiny on those benefiting from preferential treatment. The most notable mandate for preferences is that of affirmative action. The subject of executive orders signed by U.S. Presidents Kennedy, Johnson, and Nixon, affirmative action began as a well-intentioned (and temporary) rectifier of past injustices. Hardly just an American problem, preferential placements, and subsequent cries of reverse discrimination are argued over in many countries.[53] Thomas Sowell, of the Hoover Institution, laments the results of affirmative action in the United States with:

> It was after the civil rights movement itself began to move away from this concept of equal treatment of all individuals and toward the concept of equalized outcomes for groups, that a backlash against affirmative action set in and grew over the years.[54]

In *Mismatch: How Affirmative Action is Hurting the Students its Intended to Help and Why Universities Won't Admit It*, UCLA law professor Rick Sander and Brookings fellow Stuart Taylor provide a strong case for reforming affirmative action. The authors cite a dramatic drop in failure rates for minority students at UCLA after racial preferences were eliminated from admissions decisions. The ban on racial preferences stems from California's Proposition 209 which was passed by voter referendum in 1996. Sander and Taylor report that "the total number of black and Hispanic students receiving bachelor's degrees was the same for the five classes after Prop 209 as for the five classes before." The authors tout the ban on racial preferences resulted in "better matched students at UCLA," reducing incidences of mismatch.[55]

Gail Heriot, law professor at the University of San Diego and member of the U.S. Commission on Civil Rights, claims that affirmative action results in lower rates of college completion by blacks and Hispanics. She contends that if less qualified minority applicants (that currently get preferential admissions treatment) attended less select institutions, there would be more (in absolute terms) minority engineers, doctors, and lawyers—just not as many from the most elite institutions.[56]

Richard Sander continues to press his critics for their disinclination to acknowledge empirical evidence regarding mismatch. In a 2015 *Wall Street Journal* opinion piece, he reiterates his position with:

> The mismatch theory is not about race. It is about admissions preferences, full stop. Mismatch can affect students who receive preferential admission based on athletic prowess, low socioeconomic status, or alumni parents. An important finding of mismatch research is that when one controls for the effect of admissions preferences, racial differences in college performance largely disappear.[57]

Bamboo Ceiling?[58]

Many Asian American groups have been at a distinct disadvantage with regard to college admission. Dozens of Asian American organizations filed complaints with the U.S. Department of Education against Harvard for racial discrimination.[59] The truth is that as a group, Asian Americans have better test scores and grades than their white, black, and Hispanic counterparts. Asian American students come from a culture where education, college readiness, and aspirations are valued higher than in other demographic groups. Sure, family income and parents' education have some influence, but hard work and the prioritizing of education have driven the imbalance in the metrics.

Citing data from the National Center for Education Statistics, *The Economist* reported the percentage of Asian Americans enrolled in 2014 at Cal Berkeley was 41 percent, and 44 percent at the California Institute of Technology. Both are sharp increases compared to figures prior to Proposition 209.[60]

Outside of the ivory tower, Asian Americans do well professionally and economically. However, they appear underrepresented within top executive ranks. A report by Ascend, a Pan-Asian professional organization, claimed Asian Americans at several tech companies (Google, Intel, Hewlett-Packard, LinkedIn, and Yahoo), comprised "27% of professionals, 19% of managers, and 14% of executives."[61] Whites meanwhile, make up over 60 percent of professional positions in these same firms, roughly 75 percent of the managers, and a more disproportionate 80 percent of executives.

Asian Americans fare worse in the C-suite of Fortune 500 firms, garnering just 2 percent of those coveted CEO posts in 2014. According to Guilford College's Richard Zweigenhaft, the number of women CEOs in the Fortune 500 has risen sixfold in the last 14 years, and now stands at 24 (4.8 percent).[62] The *Harvard Business Review* recently pegged female CEOs at just 3 percent of the S&P 1200.[63] Asian Americans account for only 10 of over 3,000 college presidents in the United States. Relatedly, *The Economist* reports that in 2014, 11 percent of law firm associates were of Asian descent while just 3 percent of law firm partners were Asian.[64]

The Economist also points to a higher incidence of political leadership of Indo-Americans over Chinese Americans. Importantly, Indian immigrants emanate from the world's largest democracy, while Chinese immigrants were influenced by a home country soaked in Confucianism and communist rule—hardly fertile training grounds for politicking or chest pounding bravado. So yes, not surprisingly, culture matters a lot.

Given the unevenly distributed leadership demographics of corporate, higher education, legal, and political realms, is it practical to assume that these institutions would perform better if leadership demographics were more reflective of the general population, or at least be more diverse—racially, ethnically, or gender-wise? The short answer is probably no. Why would it matter?

I fail to see how the performance of the organizations in any of the domains just discussed will be improved by making the racial, ethnic, or gender profiles of the organizations and their respective leadership more reflective of the general population. Will new demographic distribution paradigms in these institutions bring other benefits? Probably. Will higher representation of minorities in senior ranks connote, on the surface, more fairness? Yes. Are many of the disproportional statistics presented in this chapter reflective of past injustices? Absolutely. But bear in mind that much of the data can be explained by obvious as well as subtle sociocultural factors, pipeline issues, geography, and network effects. Diversity efforts that try for home runs in terms of improving performance outcomes are often overly ambitious and lack objectivity. Many diversity mandates are uneven in scope and not representative of a truly meritocratic society.

I have used a combination of broad strokes and specific empirical evidence in my criticism of many inaccurate claims of diversity's dividends. This chapter is far from a complete accounting of this contentious topic. Diversity is too complex to treat with media sound bites and sweeping rationalizations void of evidence and transparency. Generally speaking, diversity's impact on performance is mixed at best. The ramifications on policy, organizations, and people are too important to blindly accept shallow dogma on this issue.

As academics are fond of saying, further study is recommended.

Contra Maxims for Diversity

Avoid using and identifying with stereotypes. Focus on relevant diversity.[65] Diversity of thought and perspective matter. Leverage diversity—in all its forms. Respect differences. Be mindful of biases. Individual–organizational fit is a two-way street. Fitting in is everyone's responsibility. We all have to *get* each other, and sometimes just leave each other alone. Sometimes, diversity improves performance, and sometimes it doesn't.

Notes

1. U.S. Census Bureau, "Men in Nursing Occupations: American Community Survey Highlight Report," 2013, http://www.census.gov/people/io/files/Men_in_Nursing_Occupations.pdf (accessed Jan 22, 2016).

2. Sports Reference, LLC, "NBA League Averages," 2015, http://www.basketball-reference.com/leagues/NBA_stats.html (accessed Jan 22, 2016).

3. Richard Lapchick and Angelica Guiao, "The 2015 Racial and Gender Report Card: National Basketball Association," The Institute for Diversity and Ethics in Sport at the University of Central Florida, 2015, http://nebula.wsimg.com/6e1489cc3560e1e1a2fa88e3030f5149?AccessKeyId=DAC3A56D8FB782449D2A&disposition=0&alloworigin=1 (accessed May 22, 2016).

4. *The Atlantic*, "Silicon Valley Insiders Poll," Nov 2015: 76–81. Note: The poll uses a panel of "101 executives, innovators, and thinkers." Selection methodology for the panel is not stipulated, but names of respondents are provided.

5. Knowledge at Wharton, "'Gender Equality by Design': Building a More Inclusive (and Productive) Workplace," *Knowledge @ Wharton*, 24 Mar 2016, http://knowledge.wharton.upenn.edu/article/gender-equality-design-building-inclusive-productive-workplace/?utm_source=kw_newsletter&utm_medium=email&utm_campaign=2016-03-24 (accessed Mar 26, 2016).

6. Katherine Williams and Charles O'Reilly, "Demography and Diversity: A Review of 40 years of Research," in Barry Staw and Robert Sutton (Eds.) *Research in Organizational Behavior* 20: 77–140 (Greenwich, CT: JAI Press, 1998); Jeffrey Pfeffer, "Organizational Demography," in Barry Straw and Larry Cummings (Eds.), *Research in Organizational Behavior* 5: 299–357 (Greenwich, CT: JAI Press, 1983).

7. Joshua Sacco and Neal Schmitt, "A Dynamic Multilevel Model of Demographic Diversity and Misfit Effects," *Journal of Applied Psychology* 90, no. 2 (2005): 203–231; Williams and O'Reilly, "Demography and Diversity"

8. Tyler Cowen, *Creative Destruction: How Globalization is Changing the World's Cultures* (New York, NY: Basic Books, 2002).

9. Thomas Sowell, *The Thomas Sowell Reader* (New York, NY: Basic Books, 2011), 272.

10. Raymond Taras (Ed.), *Challenging Multiculturalism: European Models of Diversity* (Edinburgh, Scotland: Edinburgh University Press, 2013).

11. Cowen, *Creative Destruction*, 134–135.

12. Ibid., 16.

13. Vivian Hunt, Dennis Layton and Sara Prince, *Diversity Matters* (McKinsey & Company, 2015), http://www.mckinsey.com/Insights/Organization/Why_diversity_matters (accessed Jan 16, 2016).

14. Ibid.

15. Ibid., 1.

16. Scott Page, "Making the Difference: Applying a Logic of Diversity," *Academy of Management Perspectives* 21, no. 4 (2007): 6–20.

17. Ibid.

18. Ibid., 14.

19. Adam Bryant, "Fostering a Respectful Clash of Ideas," *The New York Times*, 24 Jan 2015, BU2.

20. Bloomberg Television, "Bloomberg Go," 9 Mar 2016, http://on.aol.com/video/comstock%3A-we-need-more-diversity-in-the-boardroom-519560692

21. Martin Davidson, *The End of Diversity as We Know It* (San Francisco, CA: Berrett-Koehler, 2011), 191.

22. Thomas Kochan, Katerina Bezrukova, Robin Ely, Susan Jackson, Aparna Joshi, Karen Jehn, Jonathan Leonard, David Levine and David Thomas, "The Effects of Diversity on Business Performance: Report of the Diversity Network," *Human Resource Management* 42, no. 1 (2003): 3–21. Note: Authors represented the following institutions: MIT, Wharton School of the University of Pennsylvania, Harvard Business School, Rutgers University, University of Illinois at Urbana-Champaign, and the University of California, Berkeley.

23. Ibid., 16.

24. Ibid., 18.

25. Ibid.

26. Michele Jayne and Robert Dipboye, "Leveraging Diversity to Improve Business Performance: Research Findings and Recommendations for Organizations," *Human Resource Management* 42, no. 4 (2004): 409–424.

27. Ibid.

28. Cristian Dezso and David Gaddis Ross, "Does Female Representation in Top Management Improve Firm Performance? A Panel Data Investigation," *Strategic Management Journal* 33, (2012): 1072–1089.

29. Ibid., 1085.

30. Iris Bohnet, *What Works: Gender Equality by Design* (Cambridge, MA: Belknap Press, 2016), 228.

31. Orlando Richard, "Racial Diversity, Business Strategy, and Firm Performance: A Resource-based View," *Academy of Management Journal* 43, no. 2 (2000): 164–177.

32. Sujin Horwitz and Irwin Horwitz, "The Effects of Team Diversity on Team Outcomes: A Meta-analytic Review of Team Demography," *Journal of Management* 33, no.6 (2007): 987–1015.

33. Nagaraj Sivasubramaniam, S. Jay Liebowitz, and Conway Lackman, "Determinants of New Product Development Team Performance: A Meta-analytic Review," *Journal of Product Innovation Management* 29, no. 5 (2012): 803–820.

34. Donna Chrobot-Mason Nicholas Aramovich, "The Psychological Benefits of Creating an Affirming Climate of Workplace Diversity," *Group and Organization Management* 38, no.6 (2013): 659–689.

35. Note: Search of publication titles form all Academy of Management journals and proceedings, by date constraints, using research title as key search field. *Gender* was used as gender indicator while *race* and *racial* were used as markers for race-focused studies. http://journals.aom.org/search.(accessed Jan 22, 2016).

36. *Makers: Women Who Make America* (Washington, DC: Kunhardt McGee Productions, Public Broadcasting Service, 2013, WETA-TV).

37. Deborah Rhode and Amanda Packel, "Director Notes: Diversity on Corporate Boards: How Much 'Difference' Does Difference Make?" The Conference Board, Feb 2015, No. DN-V7N2. www.conference-board.org/director notes.

38. Ibid., 4.

39. Ibid.

40. Corinne Post and Kris Byron, "Women on Boards and Firm Financial Performance: A Meta-analysis," *Academy of Management Journal* 58, no. 5 (2015): 1563.

41. Ibid.

42. Jessica Canning, Maryam Haque and Yimeng Wang, *Women at the Wheel: Do Female Executives Drive Start-up Success?* (New York, NY: Dow Jones & Company, 2012), 3, http://www.dowjones.com/privatemarkets/pm_download.asp.

43. Ibid., 21.

44. Ibid., 32.

45. Ibid., 12.

46. Ira Irene Bergstrom, "Gender Differences in Leadership Are a Myth," Committee for Gender Balance and Diversity in Research, 1 Nov 2013, http://eng.kifinfo.no/nyhet/vis.html?tid=83367 (accessed Jan 27, 2016).

47. Sowell, *The Thomas Sowell Reader* (New York, NY: Basic Books, 2011), 264.

48. David Sacks and Peter Thiel, *The Diversity Myth: Multiculturalism and Political Correctness on Campus* (Oakland, CA: The Independent Institute, 1998).

49. Ibid., 117.

50. Ibid., 105.

51. Daphne Patai and Harvey Silverglate, "From Suppressing to Compressing," *Inside Higher Ed*, 2016, https://www.insidehighered.com/views/2016/04/25/new-diversity-requirements-umass-amherst-compel-speech-and-belief-essay (accessed May 2, 2016).

52. Aldous Huxley, *Proper Studies* (London, United Kingdom: Chatto & Windus, 1929), 132.

53. Sowell, *The Thomas Sowell Reader* (New York, NY: Basic Books, 2011).

54. Ibid., 300.

55. Richard Sander and Stuart Taylor, *Mismatch: How Affirmative Action Hurts the Students It's Intended to Help and Why Universities Won't Admit It* (New York, NY: Basic Books, 2012), 8.

56. Intelligence Squared U.S., "Debate: Affirmative Action on Campus Does More Harm than Good," 27 Feb 2014, http://www.intelligen-cesquaredus.org/debates/past-debates/item/1054-affirmative-action-on-campus-does-more-harm-than-good (accessed Jan 22, 2016).

57. Richard Sander, "How Colleges Make Racial Disparities Worse," *The Wall Street Journal* 18 Dec 2015, A17.

58. *The Economist*, "The Model Minority is Losing Patience," Oct 3–9, 2015, 23–25.

59. Ibid.

60. Ibid.

61. Ibid., 25.

62. Ibid.

63. *Harvard Business Review*, "Interaction: The Best Performing CEOs in the World," Jan–Feb 2016, 22.

64. *The Economist*, "The Model Minority"

65. Scott Page, "Making the Difference," 16.

CHAPTER 5

Competitive Advantage is Necessary to Compete

Adapt or perish, now as ever, is nature's inexorable imperative.
—H.G. Wells, *Mind at the End of its Tether*

Every man, as long as he does not violate the laws of justice, is left perfectly free to pursue his own interest his own way, and to bring both his industry and capital into competition with those of any other man, or order of men.
—Adam Smith, *An Inquiry into the Nature and Causes of the Wealth of Nations*

The ideal of competitive advantage is exalted, overprotected, worn out, and contextually misused like no other strategic management concept. Given that the base concept is so wildly misunderstood, you can bet that the inflated management maxim that claims *Competitive advantage is necessary to compete* is overripe for criticism.

My premise on competitive advantage is contrarian yet very simple: Precious few organizations have one! Now, it's not that I don't believe in the concept of competitive advantage or its phenomenal power when exploited in the marketplace. On the contrary, a true competitive advantage should be the envy of all who compete—not necessarily the goal, but certainly the envy. However, when the ideal of competitive advantage is rolled into the management maxim *Competitive advantage is necessary to compete*, we encounter serious issues with the truth and real-world pragmatism.

Before proceeding with this entrenched and ubiquitous maxim, I must first set some ground rules as to what constitutes a competitive advantage. Much of the misunderstanding about competitive advantage lies with the vagueness of the term's explicit and tacit meanings. Referencing numerous texts that have leaned on the strategy parlance of Harvard Business School's Michael Porter, a competitive advantage is "what sets the organization apart from others and provides it with a distinct edge for meeting customer or client needs in the marketplace. The essence of formulating strategy is choosing how the organization will be different."[1] Consequently, this phantom distinctiveness misleads many into thinking they have a competitive advantage.

Strategy scholar Jay Barney defined competitive advantage more formally, citing that a firm achieves it "when it is able to create more economic value than rival firms." This economic value is the customer's perception of value, which is the difference between the perceived benefits and the costs incurred by the customer.[2] In other words, a firm possessing a competitive advantage is offering a distinctively higher value (real or perceived) to customers than these customers can get from competitors.

Most strategic management experts stress the attribute of inimitability with regard to competitive advantage, meaning the distinctive edge that a firm possesses cannot be readily copied. This in turn yields a continued competitive advantage. Thus, if a firm is able to protect its distinct ability to offer the lowest prices (by being the lowest cost producer), provide the best customer service, operate the most effective distribution system, or possess patent-protected and superior product designs, then this firm will be more suited to achieve superior economic results over time.

However, most organizations do not have an inimitable edge yet they are still successful competitors. These firms routinely win customers and eke out revenue, profits, and market share—albeit not overwhelmingly— but they survive nonetheless. Scores of firms compete at the microevent level, one transaction and customer at a time.

For example, in lodging, Marriott and Hilton each offer a range of lodging choices, but neither has a compelling, distinctive attribute that makes them superior. For automobiles, Ford, Nissan, and Honda all offer good quality cars, but it's not difficult to find comparable models across each firm's product lines. Casual dining is jammed with similar options across categories, depending on how long you want to wait for your food and how much you are willing to pay. Department stores such as Target, Kohl's, JC Penney, and Macy's all offer quality merchandise, and it is often on sale. All of the above companies do lots of little things well, but you would be hard pressed to name an inimitable advantage possessed by any of them.

Where does a *sustainable* competitive advantage stand in this discussion? When escalating the maxim to include the sustainable kind, the number of competitively advantageous firms quickly drops to the endangered species category. A truly sustainable competitive advantage is the pinnacle of strategic and general management. It is often represented by a strong first mover advantage, protected product differentiation, extreme brand loyalty, or some interdivisional alchemy that borders on corporate sorcery. This alchemy may be better described as a unique combination of activities within the company, which we'll discuss a bit later. Nevertheless, most true competitive advantages are temporary. Successful market performers tend to attract attention that stirs competitors to match the frontrunners in some way.

For thought leaders in this domain, the classic rock star of the strategy set would have to be Michael Porter. His early, landmark books included *Competitive Strategy* (1980) and *Competitive Advantage* (1985). Porter introduced us to the enduring Competitive Forces Model, which includes these five industry forces: rivalry of firms, threat of substitutes, threat of new entrants, power of suppliers, and power of buyers. Porter also delineated his three generic strategies of cost leadership, focus, and differentiation. A third hallmark contribution, described initially in 1985s *Competitive Advantage*, was the widely adopted Value Chain Analysis. Using the Value Chain Analysis, a thorough understanding of a firm's critical activities and support functions could reveal both shortcomings and sources of actionable value.

Porter's strategic thinking proclivity coincided with a boom in the strategy consulting industry, most notably served by the big three firms: McKinsey, Bain, and Boston Consulting Group.[3] This was a perfect storm of sorts where economists and strategy theorists sought to explain phenomena, consultants sought lucrative contracts, and large corporations sought help in coping with more competitive and globalized markets.

Competition-centric practitioners such as management icon Jack Welch, the former General Electric (GE) CEO, embraced the competitive advantage mantra head on. Welch once growled that "If you don't have a competitive advantage, don't compete."[4] This proclamation is indicative of how this faux maxim achieved such enduring and lofty status in management circles. Heck, if Jack Welch espouses it, it must be true! Normally I would say that is the case. However, in reality, there would be so few firms in existence if they stopped competing due to the absence of a competitive advantage. Perhaps Welch's legendary strategic conviction that every GE business be either the #1 or #2 market share player (or shed the business) has skewed his outlook with regard to competition. In reality, if most CEOs thought this way, we would have a world filled with monopolies. There would be no third, fourth, and certainly no tenth competitor in many industries. Thankfully for customers, both consumer and industrial, this is not the case.

An outlier mindset regarding competitive philosophy is held by PayPal cofounder and venture capitalist Peter Thiel. Along with Blake Masters, Thiel wrote the recent best seller *Zero to One* that laid out their vision for market leadership from a tech start-up perspective. In a contrarian stance, the authors claimed that new enterprises should not be disruptive. Upstart firms should instead focus on a small market and seek to dominate it with a superior offering. Avoiding crowded, established markets is one of their central tenets for success.

However, for most entrepreneurs this is essentially fairytale land. It reminds me of a bit done by the actor/comedian Steve Martin. As a young standup comic, Martin posed a tantalizing proposition during a *Saturday Night Live* episode: "You can be a millionaire, and never pay taxes!" You say, "Steve, how can *I* be a millionaire, and never pay taxes?" Martin's cheeky reply was, "First, get a million dollars."[5] Similarly, in *Zero to One*, Thiel and Masters seem to be goading would-be entrepreneurs to simply go out and start the next Google, Facebook, PayPal, or Tesla. Sure thing, sounds easy enough. What are you waiting for?

Survey Findings

In 2005, I surveyed the leaders of 127 organizations that included small manufacturers (such as machine shops and light industrial manufacturing), health care providers (community hospitals and nursing care facilities), and public school systems. Not surprisingly, 79 percent of manufacturing CEOs felt they had a competitive advantage, 86 percent of health care leaders claimed to have a competitive advantage, and 53 percent of school system honchos believed they possessed a competitive advantage.[6]

When asked what specifically was the organization's competitive advantage, those in the small manufacturing group mentioned the following: unique technology; skilled employees; low cost production; innovation; engineering; partnerships; marketing channels; reliability; brand name; and customer service. A sampling of reasons for a competitive advantage in the health care group contained reputation; great clinicians and staff; niche programs; diverse programs; only game in town; location; small, caring and focused; culture; customer satisfaction; and best clinical practices. The education group, with the lowest incidence of self-reporting a competitive advantage, elicited the following responses: student-focused; dedicated employees; exclusive niche; sole provider; worthy mission; continuous improvement; excellent teachers; and small classes.

While all of the above responses are admirable strengths to use when competing, only the geographic exclusivity of the public schools and a few of the health care facilities represent an enduring (yet not unthreatened) competitive advantage. I contend that the manufacturing firms and the majority of health care providers are successful, at least in the near term, because of their capabilities to adapt and compete on a daily basis. For example, they must continually nurture and replace employees. They must reorient their technology, manufacturing techniques, partnerships, and pathways to market in order to stay competitive. These organizations are unlikely to possess an inimitable advantage. They compete separately and continually for each customer, patient, deal, or contract on a situational, case-by-case basis. Impressively, they do this day after day.

The Kauffman Firm Survey, a national probability survey of new businesses in the United States, inquired about competitive advantage thinking of firm founders. The survey's principle investigator, entrepreneurship scholar Scott A. Shane, writes that "only 63 percent of the founders of new businesses reported that their new business had a competitive advantage."[7] Given the expected positive bias from founders' optimism, this is a remarkable finding. Perhaps the realities of the competitive marketplace have accurately informed the outlook of these entrepreneurs.

A Grocer's Tale

Some companies are commonly identified with the wrong competitive advantage. You may recall the feel-good story of the Market Basket grocery chain located throughout New England. In the summer of 2014, a bitter boardroom battle erupted over control and management of this private firm. The company has a long history of family disputes. Boardroom and shareholder power was shifting to settle old scores. Widely respected CEO Arthur T. DeMoulas (not to be confused with his boardroom rival and first cousin Arthur S. DeMoulas) was ousted and replaced with two co-CEOs.[8] Employees and customers (me included) turned out in droves to support Arthur T. and his quest to preserve the *Market Basket Way*. For decades, the firm had been known for low prices and excellent employee relations among its full-timers.

Employee solidarity, walk-outs, and a customer boycott eventually crippled store revenue. Several public rallies were held to demand that Arthur T. be reinstated as CEO so that business could return to normal. Arthur T. eventually succeeded with a buyout. Stores reopened and customers happily flocked back (again, me included). This story is often told with customer and employee loyalty heralded as the competitive advantages, with Arthur T.'s management style and trustworthiness being the impetus for that employee loyalty. And yes, there is tremendous employee loyalty at this company, demonstrably shown when Arthur T. was fired and then reappointed. Scores of employees refused to go back to work unless Arthur T. was back in charge.

However, the underlying competitive advantage for Market Basket is not loyalty nor is it trusted management, admirable and effective as these attributes may be. Market Basket's real competitive advantage is low prices. No full-line grocer in the region comes close (or desires to come close) to matching Market Basket's prices. Customers boycotted the chain and showed up at rallies because they wanted their low price grocery chain to stay as is, myself included. Market Basket does have a competitive advantage with their low prices. They can maintain this posture because management has the discipline to resist growth beyond their friendly, regional confines. As Michael Porter pointed out long ago, "The growth imperative is hazardous to strategy."[9] Market Basket, under Arthur T. DeMoulas, has thus far shown the discipline to make trade-offs to choose which markets to focus on.

Everything is Temporary

Michael Porter saw the difficulty with the sustainability aspect of competitive advantage, warning in *Competitive Advantage*, "Since barriers to imitation are never insurmountable, however, it is usually necessary for a firm to offer a moving target to its competitors by investing in order to improve its position."[10]

More recently, Columbia University's Rita Gunther McGrath has taken up the mantra of *transient* competitive advantage as a logical extension of Harvard's Clayton Christiansen and his timeless provocations from his book *The Innovator's Dilemma*. Both authors emphasize how an organization can be trapped in a currently successful competitive advantage, resisting the signal to migrate from one product platform to another, for example.

Christiansen pointed out the perils of Digital Equipment's strict adherence to its then lucrative minicomputer business in the 1980s, which resulted in the firm missing out on the burgeoning PC industry. Digital Equipment did not want to proactively destroy their margins in the near term. McGrath continues the case study tradition in this domain but also points to traditional strategic frameworks as the apparent dinosaurs. Akin to blasphemy in traditional competitive strategy circles, McGrath claims companies should embrace the transient competitive advantage approach and abandon historical positioning stalwarts such as Porter's Five Forces, Boston Consulting Group's Growth-Share Matrix, and SWOT (Strengths, Weaknesses, Opportunities, and Threats) analysis. Heresy and shock value aside, McGrath's emphasis is on organizational speed and a discovery orientation. Refreshingly, McGrath advises companies to be more experimental, flexible, and faster at decision making. Expecting mistakes and near misses due to haste and inherent uncertainty, this discovery-minded approach preaches quick reactions and adjustments.[11]

Also reflecting the market's insistence on speed and responsiveness, the once venerable Hewlett-Packard (H-P) decided in 2015 to split into two companies. Seeing H-P lose ground to swifter aggressors like Amazon and Apple, CEO Meg Whitman remarked, "We need to be smaller, more nimble, we need to be more focused." She also noted how the marketplace was "changing at lightning speed."[12]

Similarly, Google decided in August 2015 to essentially split in two by forming Alphabet as a way to focus on noncore, moon shot initiatives. The Google case is particularly interesting, given the restructuring was done much sooner than conventional wisdom would have predicted. Time will tell if the new Google and H-P entities will produce more competitive positions and sustained growth.

Phil Rosenzweig, in his bracing classic *The Halo Effect*, recounts what he calls the *delusion of lasting success*. This delusion (there were eight others in the book), falls squarely on the elusiveness of a sustainable competitive advantage. Rosenzweig points to the poor track record of the firms celebrated in Peters and Waterman's *In Search of Excellence*, given that two-thirds of the companies profiled had marked performance drops just a few years out from their much-publicized stardom.[13] Again, this is further testament to the tenuousness of staying power with regard to competitive advantage.

Both Rosenzweig and business journalist Walter Keichel, author of the informative *Lords of Strategy*, point to the research of McKinsey's Richard Foster. Foster reported only 74 of the original Standard & Poor's (S&P) 500 blue chip firms were still in the index from 1957 to 1998. More glumly, only 12 of those remaining 74 firms outperformed the S&P index over the same period.[14] Keichel viewed the public's shock at these figures as evidence of a common malady of business book readers, which was believing in the aura of corporate persistence. In their book *Creative Destruction*, Richard Foster and Sarah Kaplan cite the tumult of market discontinuities as reason for much of the churn of blue chip firms. They refer to the perpetually overachieving company as a myth.[15]

Indeed, many assume that excellent blue chip companies will stay blue indefinitely due to their pedigree, well-executed strategies, and yes you guessed it—competitive advantages. In reality, consistency of excellence and competitive advantage are extraordinarily hard to achieve over time. Further evidence of the precariousness of corporate performance over the long haul is reflected in the work of Jim Collins. In his best seller *Good to Great*, Collins reported only 9 percent (126 firms) of 1,435 companies were able to substantially outperform market averages over 10-year periods.[16]

Mere survivability as a company is becoming more of a feat given today's competitiveness. The Boston Consulting Group's Martin Reeves and Lisanne Pueschel produced some compelling data in 2015 on corporate mortality, writing:

> Today, almost one-tenth of all public companies fail each year, a fourfold increase since 1965. The five-year exit risk for public companies traded in the U.S. now stands at 32 percent, compared with the 5 percent risk they would have faced 50 years ago.[17]

The popular 2005 book *Blue Ocean Strategy*, by INSEAD strategy professors W. Chan Kim and Renee Mauborgne, explains the importance of exploiting *unknown* (new) market spaces as blue ocean strategy. In contrast, more established markets crowded with competitors are referred to as red oceans. Citing them as representative of most industries, Kim and Mauborgne studied the automobile, computer, and movie theater industries. They concluded that there is "no permanently excellent industry" and there are "no permanently excellent companies." Kim and Mauborgne attributed shifts in competitive advantage to the ongoing delivery of "innovative value" to customers.[18]

Intel's Andy Grove, in his tech strategy chronicle *Only the Paranoid Survive*, reflected on the ups and downs of strategic inflection points. He both marveled at and lamented the shifts in competitive advantages, particularly in the semiconductor and memory chip segments, caused by industry inflection points. Grove saw the fleeting, dynamic nature of competitive advantage first hand. He recollected that "Having been both affected by strategic inflection points and having caused them, I can safely say that the former is tougher."[19]

Pretty Good at a Lot of Things

The reality of most organizations that slug it out day by day is that they are essentially not great at any one activity. They lack a distinctive, special talent or secret sauce. They are not superior to foes with regard to quality, speed to market, low-cost production, or best customer service. They are unlikely to be fortunate in possessing a proprietary design or algorithm. By definition, they do not have a competitive advantage. But alas, these firms have been in business for several years and are pretty good at a lot of different things.

Michael Porter, while emphasizing the importance of fit for individual activities within a company, stressed the need for management to embody a seemingly holistic and systemic approach to creating competitive advantage. In his Harvard Business Review (HBR) article *What is Strategy?*, Porter states that "Competitive advantage grows out of the entire system of activities," and further expounded that "Strategy is the creation of a unique and valuable position, involving a different set of activities."[20]

Now we can see the evolution of competitive advantage becoming less reliant on narrow one-hit-wonders such as a design patent or lowest cost via economies of scale, with the latter often resulting in a disastrous race to the bottom. Competing on price alone can be a ruinous undertaking. Porter viewed market competitiveness based solely on operational efficiencies as "mutually destructive" and no longer a viable basis for competitive advantage.[21]

Further signaling the need to create competitive magic from the mundane across multiple business units, the noted duo of C.K. Prahalad and Gary Hamel wrote, "The real sources of advantage are to be found in management's ability to consolidate corporate wide technologies and production skills into competencies that empower individual businesses to adapt quickly to changing opportunities."[22] Note the emphasis on the more intangible attributes of management prowess, time (i.e., speed to market), and change. Compare this to earlier, more unidimensional measures of competitive advantage such as lowest production cost. The metrics for ascertaining competitive advantage have indeed gotten a lot fuzzier.

For a single business unit example (not part of a conglomerate) employing a systemic competitive strategy, Southwest Airlines provides an excellent case study. Many often point to Southwest's fun, quirky flight attendants as a possible competitive advantage. However, while they may sing and joke more than flight attendants from other airlines, you are more likely to book your flight with Southwest due to cost, cities served, and scheduling. There appears to be no real difference among domestic carriers regarding inflight experiences, most attendants are kind and helpful, and most coach seats are uncomfortable. Customers would rather not pay an extra $200 or add 2 hours to their trip for a more entertaining set of announcements.

Southwest is particularly competitive via a combination of activities that includes high degree of sameness of aircraft, high equipment utilization, short point-to-point routing (fewer connections and baggage handling), limited perks, and reasonable prices. This coordination of activities helps Southwest keep its cost structure under control. While not being all things to all people, Southwest has executed very well while being pretty good at several things—in a tough industry.

Walmart is another superb example of a combinative competitive advantage. Assuming they have one, what would you say is Walmart's competitive advantage? The most common answer to this question is low prices. The legendary Sam Walton himself supported this view by saying, "Control your expenses better than your competition. This is where you can always find the competitive advantage."[23] Indeed, solid old school advice. But contemporary market leadership needs to go beyond today's givens of operational efficiencies.

So how does Walmart manage this low-cost leadership position? Essentially, Walmart is a relentless executor of a strategy focused on information technology (IT) coupled with state-of-the-art supply chain management (SCM) techniques, of which Walmart was an early adopter. Combine the IT and SCM expertise with their obvious economies of scale power and you have the ability to offer the lowest prices. Again, Walmart senior management has been able to coordinate a complex set of activities in an effective, disciplined manner. Even as the massive, full-line death star of discount merchandising, Walmart does not try to be all things to all people.

For a personal account of the fleeting nature of competitive advantage, I recall my days as a product manager in the sports medicine and arthroscopic surgery market. Working for Smith & Nephew in the late 1980s and 1990s, I was fascinated at the strength of our market position. We were the market share leader in motorized arthroscopic resection and bone debridement, enjoying the fruits of our first mover advantage in a growing market trending to less invasive surgery. Success in this market began attracting good competitors eager for a share of the spoils in this space.

Smith & Nephew's competitive advantage was its large installed base and a cadre of new surgeons being trained on our equipment. We made good, reliable products and also had an excellent commission-based distributor network full of motivated sales reps. Eventually, pricing pressure ensued, competitors gained traction, and new technologies clamored for customer attention—all in the wake of tumultuous health care reform and customer (hospital) consolidation. This market certainly had its share of discontinuities. After nearly 20 dominant years, this division of Smith & Nephew was still successful and extremely capable in many aspects, but so too were other brands. Competitors such as Stryker, ConMed's Linvatec, and Arthrocare (purchased by Smith & Nephew in 2014) eroded Smith & Nephew's robust yet unsustainable market fiat.

Competitive Advantage as a Medieval Moat

Like American football, our business lexicon is chock full of military terminology. Examples of these common terms and phrases include product launch, guerilla marketing, territory acquisition, industrial espionage, flanking maneuver, retaliatory pricing, sales force on the front lines, and hostile takeover. A term used with particular resonance in competitive advantage analysis is that of a moat. Primarily thought of as medieval defensive trenches, moats were often filled with water and surrounded the ramparts and parapets of castles.

Morningstar, the investment rating service, uses the metaphor of a moat to signify the presence, strength, and potential sustainability of a competitive advantage.[24] Although Morningstar relies heavily on historical financial performance, it also evaluates a firm's competitiveness by reviewing the industry's competitive structure. Morningstar uses the following five characteristics (a moat rubric of sorts) to determine the strength of competitive advantage:

> Network Effect. Competitive advantage is enhanced as more users get involved, such as with Facebook and EBay.

Intangible Assets. Intellectual property, such as patents and trademarks, brand equity, and licenses bring value to the firm's competitive standing. Starbucks and Apple are two examples that exhibit considerable strength with this metric.

Cost Advantage. A lower cost basis than competitors offers the opportunity for enhanced margins and profitability. Walmart shines in this regard.

Switching Costs. Prohibitive costs may be faced by customers if they choose to switch brands. These costs include training, spare parts, and system integration requirements. Firms such as Paychex and Autodesk involve high switching costs for customers, whereby Starbucks would entail none.

Efficient Scale. A small number of firms may be adequately serving a niche market, thereby precluding additional competitors from encroaching.[25] An example of this type of market would be package delivery, dominated by United Parcel Service and Federal Express.

While the framework for assigning competitive advantage status to a firm may seem adequate, it is worth a look to see what moat ratings specific companies have received. Moat types include NONE: signifying the firm has no competitive advantage; NARROW: denoting a firm with a limited competitive advantage, perhaps lasting up to 10 years; and WIDE: connoting a robust, defensible, and often sustainable competitive advantage, with superior returns foreseeable for up to 20 years.[26] A sample of firms and their respective moat ratings is provided in Table 5.1.

Table 5.1 offers a glimpse into Morningstar's stock analysis rating system. It appears Morningstar can rationalize a moat rating in any direction based on their interpretation of the moat rubric. One cannot help but wonder how Starbucks secures a wide moat while Boeing and Apple are rated with narrow moats. Granted, Morningstar rightfully assigns both Boeing and Apple wide *quantitative* (secondary) moat ratings, but to think a coffee shop is better defended than a leading aerospace giant is surprising. Also, given Apple's $200 billion in cash on its balance sheet, one would think that all that money could buy Apple a wider moat!

Table 5.1 *A sample of firms and moat ratings. Source note: Moat ratings, market capitalizations, and EPS (earnings per share) growth percentages are from Morningstar Equity Analyst Reports for each company, dated from June 1 to June 15, 2015*

Moat type	Company	Market cap (billions)	5-year EPS annual growth rate %	10-year EPS annual growth %	Rationale for moat rating
None	Panera	$4.5B	19.0%	18.2%	Crowded casual dining segment; no switching costs; low barriers to entry
None	Macy's	$22.8B	38.4%	8.1%	No switching costs; highly competitive discretionary retail sector
None	Tesla	$31.7B	–	–	High investment risk profile with uncertain technology acceptance
None	Dollar General	$23B	27.2%	12.9%	Very competitive space; hard to differentiate; no switching costs
Narrow	Netflix	$37.8	16.9%	29.2%	Over 50 million subscribers; massive data sets and cloud integration; lots of hype and unknowns
Narrow	Apple	$741B	37.8%	62.4%	Short product competing cycles and absence of switching costs
Narrow	Boeing	$97B	31.6%	12.7%	Significant barriers to entry; global duopoly in large commercial jets; strong customer relationships
Narrow	Federal Express	$54B	84.8%	9.4%	Efficient scale; barriers to entry; and network effect; U.S. duopoly with United Parcel Service
Wide	Starbucks	$77B	38.9%	19.0%	Intangible value of brand; economies of scale
Wide	Walmart	$239B	6.1%	7.6%	Massive economies of scale and reputation as low-cost provider
Wide	Google	$363B	19.6%	39.4%	Online search dominance; network effect; technology reinvestment

Netflix presents another perplexing case when using moats for determining competitive advantage. Morningstar's Equity Analyst Report states that Netflix is leveraging its massive data set "across its multiple offerings in multiple ways to derive sustainable competitive advantages."[27] Apparently, Morningstar analysts feel this sustainment will last only 10 years, not 20. Speaking of which, a 20-year projection of outsized returns is an aggressive call considering market uncertainties and discontinuities. Fortunately for Morningstar, it can change its moat ratings whenever it chooses. Nevertheless, it is hard to fathom how some firms (i.e., their senior management) get the faith of Morningstar to sustain their advantages much further out than other capable firms and managers.

While Morningstar is keen on ascertaining company performance (and by default management's performance), the moat framework does not include a distinct evaluator of how well management coordinates any internal set of activities. Additionally, moat analysis does not attempt to codify intangible measurements of speed and adaptation, which are increasingly cited by practitioners and scholars as being integral to competitive advantage. Perhaps the moat analysis framework is too traditional. A revised model that better incorporates a firm's human capital, nimbleness, and ability to compete at the microlevel may be more suitable in dynamic markets.

In closing the discussion on competitive advantage, note that very few firms strike gold with a one-trick pony competitive advantage. Successful companies in the future will be smart, fast, and change-oriented. If you are fortunate enough to have a real competitive advantage, be mindful that in its current form, it is temporary.

Contra Maxims for Competitive Advantage

Competitive advantages are rare, endangered, and temporary. Organizations must experiment, learn, and adapt quickly to stay competitive. Manage *everything* well!

Notes

1. Richard Daft, *Management, 10th ed.* (Mason, OH: South-Western, Cengage Learning, 2012); John Pearce and Richard Robinson,

Strategic Management: Formulation, Implementation and Control, 8th ed. (New York, NY: McGraw-Hill Education, 2003).

2. Jay Barney, *Gaining and Sustaining Competitive Advantage, 4th ed.* (Upper Saddle River, NJ: Prentice Hall, 2011), 15.

3. Walter Kiechel, *The Lords of Strategy: The Secret Intellectual History of the New Corporate World* (Boston, MA: Harvard Business Press, 2010).

4. Stratford Sherman and Cynthia Hutton, "Inside the Mind of Jack Welch," *Fortune*, 27 Mar 1989, http://archive.fortune.com /magazines/fortune/fortune_archive/1989/03/27/71783/index .htm?iid=sr-link1 (accessed 31, 2016).

5. "SNL Transcripts, Season 3, Episode 9," 21 Jan 1978. http://snltran- scripts.jt.org/77/77imono.phtml (accessed June 18, 2015).

6. Kevin Wayne, "Leader Perception of Competitive Advantage: A Regional Survey of Manufacturing, Healthcare and Education." American Society of Business and Behavioral Sciences Annual Meeting, February 21, 2009.

7. Scott Shane, *The Illusions of Entrepreneurship: The Costly Myths that Entrepreneurs, Investors, and Policy Makers Live By* (New Haven, CT: Yale University Press, 2008), 67.

8. Hilary Sargent, Adam Vaccaro and Roberto Scalese, "Two Arthurs, One Basket: The Market Basket Saga of 2014," *Boston.com*, 22 July 2014, http://www.boston.com/images/twoarthurs2.pdf (accessed June 18, 2015).

9. Michael Porter, "What is Strategy?" *Harvard Business Review* 74, no. 6 (Nov–Dec 1996): 61–78.

10. Michael Porter, *Competitive Advantage: Creating and Sustaining Superior Performance* (New York, NY: The Free Press, 1985), 20.

11. Rita Gunther McGrath, *The End of Competitive Advantage* (Boston, MA: Harvard Business Review Press, 2014).

12. Robert McMillan, "H-P Makes Its Breakup Plan Official." *Wall Street Journal*, 2 Jul 2015, B3.

13. Phil Rosenzweig, *The Halo Effect and Eight Other Business Delusions that Deceive Managers* (New York, NY: Free Press, 2014).

14. Kiechel, *Lords of Strategy.*

15. Richard Foster and Sarah Kaplan, *Creative Destruction: Why Companies that are Built to Last Underperform the Market—and How to Successfully Transform Them* (New York, NY: Crown Publishing, 2001).

16. Jim Collins, *Good to Great* (New York, NY: Harper Business, 2001), 220–222. Note: ten-year periods of substantially above average performance was preceded by a period of average or below average performance.

17. Martin Reeves and Lisanne Pueschel, "Die Another Day: What Leaders Can Do About the Shrinking Life Expectancy of Corporations," *BCG Perspectives*, 2 Jul 2015, https://www.bcgperspectives.com/content/articles/strategic-planning-growth-die-another-day/ (accessed May 4, 2016).

18. W. Chan Kim and Renee Mauborgne, *Blue Ocean Strategy: How to Create Uncontested Market Space and Make the Competition Irrelevant* (Boston, MA: Harvard Business School Press, 2005), 191–192.

19. Andy Grove, *Only the Paranoid Survive: How to Exploit the Crisis Points that Challenge Every Company* (New York, NY: Currency, 1999), 4.

20. Porter, "What is Strategy?" 68.

21. Ibid., 64.

22. C.K. Prahalad and Gary Hamel, "The Core Competence of the Corporation," *Harvard Business Review* 68, no. 3 (1990): 79–91, 81.

23. Patricia Sellers, "A Visit to Wal-mart's Home," *Fortune*, 14 Oct 2009, http://fortune.com/2009/10/14/a-visit-to-wal-marts-home/ (accessed Jun 15, 2015).

24. Morningstar, "Moats and Competitive Advantage." Investing Glossary, http://www.morningstar.com/invglossary/economic_moat.aspx (accessed Jun 19, 2015).

25. Ibid.

26. Ibid.

27. Morningstar, "Morningstar Equity Analysis Report: Netflix," 1 Jun 2015, 2, www.schwab.com (accessed July 10, 2015).

CHAPTER 6

A Business Plan is Required for Entrepreneurial Success

To succeed, planning alone is insufficient. One must improvise as well.
—Isaac Asimov, *Foundation*

Planning is an unnatural process; it is much more fun to do something. The nicest thing about not planning is that failure comes as a complete surprise, rather than being preceded by a period of worry and depression.

—Sir John Harvey-Jones

Another long-held vestige of our modern-day business vernacular has been the stubborn notion that a business plan must be constructed to ensure commercial success. In order to get your idea from the hieroglyphics scribbled on a napkin to a thriving enterprise, conventional wisdom dictates that you have to suffer through the formalities of writing a business plan.

For decades, budding entrepreneurs and inventors have been told to scribe their visions, dreams, market know-how, and business acumen into an impressive, spiral-bound treatise. Folklore has enshrined this tome as an indispensable document that every self-respecting banker, venture capitalist, angel investor, wealthy aunt, or generous uncle would insist upon prior to parting with their own or someone else's hard-earned money. Arm yourself with an impressive business plan and the money will follow—or so we have been told. Etched in the advice gospels of contemporary capitalism is the all too familiar and misleading maxim that a *Business plan is required for entrepreneurial success.*

A nascent firm's mission, strategy, business model, value proposition, management team bios, competitive positioning, intellectual property portfolio, market assumptions, sales forecast, operating plan, and financing requirements are all included in the business plan. These requisite components may also be useful for recruiting talent, securing partnerships, and planning for resource allocation.

However, numerous entrepreneurial triumphs have been accomplished without the creation of a formal business plan. Success stories sans early business plans include Bill Gates, Michael Dell, and the Google duo of Sergey Brin and Larry Page.[1] Brin and Page worked together on their search algorithms and PageRank system at Stanford for 3 years before writing a business plan. In 2000, Brin recounts events from 2 years prior in an interview with *MIT Technology Review*, saying:

> When we decided to start a company – and we actually committed to it by purchasing disks ourselves, with our own money – we spent about $15,000 on a terabyte [a million megabytes] of disks. We spread that across three credit cards. Once we did that, we wrote up a business plan and, remarkably, we have stayed close to it over the last couple years.[2]

Early and rapid success with users assured Google of access to venture capital (VC) as the company added capacity. Other entrepreneurs not starting out with a formal plan were Anita Roderick of the Body Shop retail chain and Debbie Fields with her delicious Mrs. Fields' Cookies. The early days and pre-initial public offering (IPO) successes of Frank Carney's Pizza Hut were also accomplished without a consummate plan.

I often ask small business operators and the successfully self-employed if they wrote a business plan. The answer is very often no. My local plumber with 30 years in business, 3 trucks, and 12 employees? No business plan. My home renovation contractor, so busy he can't return my phone calls, now 15 years into his enterprise? Has not got around to writing the plan yet. My electrician? Nope? How about my local neighborhood mom and pop pizza parlor, variety store, one-man computer repair service, or Certified Public Accountant (CPA)? Not one business plan among them. Bear in mind that these are not necessity entrepreneurs (those having no other choice to make ends meet). However, they are all smart, opportunistic entrepreneurs that adapted to a market demand for their services. In spite of not having a business plan, customers have found value in these enterprises.

This chapter reviews some of the many books and research studies in the business planning domain as well as insights from my own personal experience. A documentary film on venture capital is also mined for additional perspectives from the investment community. Findings consistently reveal that business plans are used primarily (and very often singularly) as fundraising implements. Lost on many in the entrepreneurial endeavors is the value of all the work done within the business plan *writing process*. Unfortunately, the knowledge gained from composing the document may be discounted or even ignored during periods of inactive fundraising.

Wannabe entrepreneurs, investors, and academics alike have duped themselves into seeing the business plan document as an end in itself. However, I contend that the process and sum of all the gritty parts of a business plan are worth more than the finished product—the impressive, full-color, gold-leafed embossed business plan reproduced on demand at the local office superstore.

The Entrepreneurial-Academic-Industrial Complex

In the wake of countless testimonials extolling the necessity of business plans, a new breed of institution has emerged into what I call the entrepreneurial-academic-industrial complex. This ambitious entity has replicated into hundreds of parochial network clusters focused on creating commercial innovation, job growth, community economic development, and at the very least some juicy public relations for local sponsors. Members of these syndicates include entrepreneurs, economic regional development centers, political opportunists (both the vote getting kind and the simply wonkish), universities and their incubators, investors, media organizations, service providers, business law folk, and consultants aplenty.

The labels used to describe these entrepreneur nurturing life forms include, but are not limited to, the following: enterprise forum, public-private partnership, entrepreneurial learning initiative, university regional economic development authority, initiative for growth, business accelerator center, entrepreneurship council, Quadruple Tri-Valley Hub for Start-up Success (OK, that one I made up), small business development network, new business development hub, and so on. I could continue, but I think you get the idea.

The aforementioned organizations are also keen sponsors of business plan contests. These events have multiplied due largely to their populist appeal, political support, entertainment and networking value, and case-based reality orientation. These gladiatorial contests are sometimes referred to as a New Venture Showcase, Venture Summit, Business Plan Competition, Shark Tank (the local, non-televised kind), Next Idea Competition, FastPitch (featuring rapid fire 3-minute elevator pitches), University Venture Challenge, International Business Model Competition, the Big Sell, and Innovation Challenge, just to name a few. These forums rarely award much needed money to the beseeching start-ups. Instead, they grant the winners some assistance via in-kind donations in the form of marketing services, lab space, conference rooms, management and legal advice, copy machine access, shared receptionist, and so on. These sponsorships generally further the cause of the donators more than the donatees via public relations and promotional bumps generated by the event. However, while these soirees usually overpromise and underdeliver, they offer exceptional networking opportunities and serve to celebrate aspirations in entrepreneurship.

While often lagging behind popular sentiments in the business community, academics have fully embraced the study of if, when, why, and by whom business plans offer value and utility. Scholars in the academic capitalism and entrepreneurial research crowds grew concerned with the advent of studies that questioned whether business plans were worth all the fuss. Concerned, because the business plan is central to the teaching of entrepreneurship at colleges and universities throughout the United States and much of the world. Imagine how uneventful the annual business plan competition would be if business plans lost their cachet.

Cutting close to the bone, the affront to the business plan's legitimacy forced many well-respected scholars to conduct their own investigations.

To their credit, academic researchers are largely true to their mission that includes the disinterested pursuit of truth in explaining environmental phenomena. And lo and behold much of the research completed in the last 15 years or so has indeed shown that the existence of comprehensive business plans has not correlated very well with successful outcomes of start-up ventures.

What the Research Tells Us

While I cannot cover the entire canon of research literature in this field, I will provide a representative sampling of what researchers have discovered recently regarding business plan efficacy. First up, in the brashly titled *Burn Your Business Plan*, David Gumpert puts forth a provocative yarn about the lack of value associated with a business plan. Gumpert not only provided an informative review of the research literature to date, he also surveyed 42 venture capitalists regarding their perceptions and use of business plans in making funding decisions.

Although Gumpert criticized the hype surrounding the business planning industry, as well as the poorly understood effectiveness of the business plan as a significant success indicator, he did not credit the *process* of business planning as well as I and others contend. Gumpert's best contribution is his insistence that entrepreneurs get into the field as soon as possible to test and prove the principles of their new business model, product, or service. He correctly stressed that a business plan without tangible feedback from real customers is not worth writing or reading.[3]

Gumpert refers to the business plan industry as a "corrupted process" hawked by academics and consultants preaching self-serving and phantom virtues of the business plan. He faults the business plan as a static document attempting to foretell the future yet not grounded in reality. While I concur with Gumpert's assertion of the business plan as a dated blueprint, I view this in a positive light. Many business professionals view their formal plans too rigidly and resist adapting to environmental realities when things don't go according to plan—which is nearly always! Consequently, I am encouraged knowing that entrepreneurs don't continually revert back to their sacred yet flawed business plan. They should adapt and improvise as conditions warrant. Although Gumpert would rather throw the business plan into the ash heap, he did praise the benefits of a hard-hitting presentation, strong set of financials, and a credible management team (especially in sales).[4]

Lastly, Gumpert railed against the consulting side of the business plan industry, claiming an entrepreneur could put that scarce money to better use by working more with customers. He also contends that the 50 to 100 hours an entrepreneur spends on the business plan could be better spent elsewhere on the opportunity.[5] This is indeed a stretch considering 50 to 100 hours is not much to ask from someone looking to borrow lots of money from investors. Suppose an entrepreneur asked you for $500,000 in seed capital and then tells you she didn't make the time (i.e., 1 week) to write a business plan. You're likely going to have doubts about this individual's level of commitment. If an entrepreneur can't spare 50 hours, an investor is unlikely to spare $50. Even if I'm only reading the executive summary and the finance section, I would like to see that the homework was done and documented. Recall your fifth grade math teacher demanding that you show your work. Nevertheless, Gumpert's research reveals a common distaste for the long-form business plan on the part of many investors.

Research published in the *Strategic Management Journal* studied 722 funding requests (mostly Internet-related ventures) submitted to one VC firm during the height of the dot.com bubble and it's bursting (1999 to 2002). The results showed the inclusion of a business plan to be a weak predictor of successful funding. This study also found business plans to be more ceremonial than communicative, and suggested that critical information about the enterprise and the market opportunity may be "learned through alternative channels." Data from the study hinted that relationships and unobserved characteristics of those involved often influence funding decisions. Just 5.4 percent of total funding requests (with or without a business plan submission) received the green light for first round funding in this sample. Needless to say, this team of researchers concluded the business plan to be of negligible value.[6]

Research done outside the United States has also given the entrepreneurial community some grim signals regarding the utility of business plans. A study in Spain using a sample of over 2,000 service-oriented start-ups found no support for business plan *quality* as a predictor of firm survival at 3 years and 6 years out.[7] Additionally, a Swedish study concluded that business plans are largely symbolic artifacts used to legitimize the entrepreneurial activities of firm founders. They also found that business plans were rarely updated or referred to after being written.[8]

In a study by noted entrepreneurship researchers led by Julian Lange of Babson College, 116 new firms were surveyed to determine if the existence of a business plan in the prelaunch phase impacted the subsequent success rate of the businesses. Lange and his team claimed that "There is no compelling reason to write a detailed business plan before opening a new business."[9] On the surface, that statement is both damning and courageous. After all, these academics and others like them have made careers out of teaching students and entrepreneurs to write formal business plans. However, this is a telling example of how semantics have gotten in the way of providing useful recommendations for practitioners. Using the business plan per se as a predictor variable for business success is often a fatal flaw in terms of the pragmatism and validity of the research.

On a positive note, in the same paper Lange and his associates countered with additional advice for entrepreneurs, including start your business with some initial projections and financials; get some practical market knowledge and traction with customers; and then write the business plan after demonstrating early progress in the field. Done this way, researchers concluded that the entrepreneur will have a stronger, evidence-based document to better position the venture for successful acquisition of capital and long-term success. Furthermore, the entrepreneurs queried in this study felt that the business plan yielded important benefits particularly in the areas of strategic planning, business model articulation, financial planning, operations planning, and the examination of critical assumptions.[10]

Some interesting work from Irish researchers demonstrated the benefits of the *exploration method* in venture creation versus the traditional business planning model. Briefly, exploration is much less prescriptive, embraces environmental uncertainty, is discovery-oriented, and veers toward the writing of business plan components as the need arises (i.e., when required by potential investors).[11]

A study in the *Journal of Small Business and Entrepreneurship* looked at 152 VC firms from around the world and found 98 percent of venture capitalists surveyed thought business plans were either important or very important. Only 31 percent of those venture capitalists invested in a firm without a business plan. Just 5 percent of respondents deemed business plans as "relics."[12] These findings lend credence to business plans as tools to bolster the chances for funding. In a separate study, Frederic Delmar and Scott Shane also found positive evidence for business planning, citing that plans lowered the odds of failure in the first 30 months, facilitated decision making due to the development of business assumptions ahead of time, and helped with goal orientation and estimates for resource requirements.[13]

A study published in 2015 in *The Journal of Business Venturing* investigated the impact of images and color as influencers of screening decisions in a business plan contest. Researchers found partial but positive support for the inclusion of images, as well as evidence that the color red may negatively impact the chances of a business plan being screened favorably. It's hard to draw too many conclusions from this quasi-experimental study, but the researchers highlighted the role of visual heuristics on the screening process. It makes sense that a busy reviewer, with only minutes to review each proposal, may rely heavily on "mental shortcuts" or "visual cues" to expedite the process.[14] To what extent are investors judging business plans by their covers? Frightfully, it appears that scented, auditory, and holographic executive summaries may be closer than we think.

One Madrid-based venture capitalist sees the eye candy bias as a serious problem. Luis Martin Cabiedes, an early stage investor, does not read business plans or watch PowerPoint pitches. He prefers interviewing founders one-on-one without the distractions to limit chances of bias.[15] Nevertheless, introductions to investors must be facilitated somehow, and referral networks carry much more clout than unsolicited mailings of glossy business plans.

Jeffrey Timmons and Stephen Spinelli, authors of my favorite text for teaching entrepreneurship (*New Venture Creation: Entrepreneurship in the 21st Century*), offer some solace to the pro-business plan camp by claiming that creation of a business plan helps with goal development and guides internal decision making.[16] Indeed, often ignored by many in the antibusiness plan faction is the value of the writing process as a booster to critical thinking. John C. Bean, a foremost writing educator, has repeatedly stressed that writing can make us better thinkers. The writing-to-learn movement embodies a process that helps us better understand the phenomena we are studying. In discussing the link between writing and critical thinking in his book *Engaging Ideas*, Bean explains:

> Quite simply, writing is both a process of doing critical thinking and a product communicating the results of critical thinking. . . . writing instruction goes sour whenever writing is perceived as a "communication skill" rather than as a process and product of critical thought.[17]

Taking Bean's lessons into account from a business plan perspective, we need to move beyond looking at the plan strictly as a communication medium aimed at impressing investors and winning contests. It is more than just a tool for legitimizing prelaunch entrepreneurial behaviors. The writing of the business plan is a chance for entrepreneurs to better understand their opportunities (and pitfalls) by thinking through scenarios, what-ifs, technological alternatives, forecasts, potential hazards, and market trends.

It should be noted that the business plan is just one variable in our efforts to understand and explain the entrepreneurship phenomenon. Entrepreneurship is an imperfect, dynamic force, often uneven and difficult to categorize. This elusive concept is even more unpredictable when studying extreme outlier cases. The Facebooks, Apples, and Googles represent the lightning strikes so many try to emulate—yet with obviously little success.

Fruitful entrepreneurship does not just make company founders successful in financial and reputational terms. A litany of societal benefits is fostered downstream from new venture achievements. These dividends include jobs for direct employees of the enterprise, revenue for local businesses serving these employees, tax revenue, contracts for suppliers, and possibly society in general due to advances made by the firm. Thus, the entrepreneurial-academic-industrial complex has tried to inculcate an environment that increases the volume of start-ups and the rate of their success. Entrepreneurship education efforts have often centered on creating better entrepreneurs. If we can identify the magic entrepreneurial traits, then maybe we can teach these skills to willing practitioners. However, this oversimplified notion of training a new type of creative class has proven to be much easier said than done.

Peter Thiel, cofounder of PayPal and an early investor in Facebook, succinctly states in his recent book *Zero to One*, "The paradox of teaching entrepreneurship is that such a formula necessarily cannot exist; because every innovation is new and unique, no authority can prescribe in concrete terms how to be innovative."[18]

Thiel is a believer in bold leaps of innovation and new ventures searching for new markets. He also sees value in planning, even waxing that "a bad plan is better than no plan."[19] He marvels at the audacious goals set and met by the likes of Steve Jobs, NASA's Apollo program, creators of the Manhattan Project, and builders of the Empire State Building and Panama Canal. Surely these great achievements did not happen without planning, budgeting, risk taking, and rigorous attention to details.

One last piece of evidence to ponder in weighing the value of a business plan for a new venture is the excellent documentary film *Something Ventured*, which chronicled the beginnings of Silicon Valley and the VC industry. In the film, released in 2011, Tom Perkins of the prestigious VC firm Kleiner Perkins confesses:

> I don't know how to write a business plan, I can only tell you how we read them, and we start at the back and if the numbers are big we look at the front to see what kind of business it is.[20]

This admission by Perkins is indicative of the truism that size often matters with regards to potential markets and its influence on positive investor sentiment.

Something Ventured also recounts how Mike Makkula, the often forgotten third founder and initial investor of Apple Computer, convinced himself to invest *while he was writing* the business plan for Apple! That's as good a testament as you may ever hear for the virtues of writing a business plan, or more accurately a testament for the business plan *writing process*. Additionally, the film tells of how Gordon Moore and Bob Noyce left Fairchild Semiconductor to form Intel, writing a one-page double-spaced business plan to help secure $2.5 million in funding. Sounds like a damn good executive summary! Lastly, *Something Ventured* also speaks to several other factors that often contribute to a start-up company's success: bootstrapping, relationship networks, perseverance, boldness, and good old-fashioned serendipity.

Nothing of Consequence goes According to Plan

Suffice it to say that the research on business plans is mixed. There is not a definitive, prototypical entrepreneurial process that guarantees success if you follow it. But lost on many is the value of preparing a business plan independent of the final document. Business planning for new ventures should be a combination of planning along with practical experience on the bench, in simulations, and most importantly, work in the field with real customers. This experience informs the planning process along the way and should make for a more compelling case for financing.

If your venture's vitality is not obvious to others, and you don't already have relationships with bona fide investors, a business plan (at least in draft form) is likely critical for fund raising. Notably, the process undertaken while writing the business plan enables critical thinking and forethought about the opportunity. The research literature paints a mixed picture for the finished document, but the business planning process comes through as a worthy prelaunch exercise that qualifies the entrepreneur to go further (certainly beyond the scribbled-on napkin).

There are caveats, however. Nobel Prize-winning psychologist Daniel Kahneman and his colleague Amos Tversky warned us about the *planning fallacy*. This delusion involves plans and forecasts that are "unrealistically close to best-case scenarios" and "could be improved by consulting the statistics of similar cases." Kahneman blames much of this on our *pervasive optimistic bias*.[21] I heed these warnings when reviewing new venture pitches at events and in the classroom. I use three rules of thumb that are negatively biased to counteract the presenter's unbridled optimism, including: the forecast is too optimistic by at least twofold; the launch date should be pushed back 6 months; and the presenters should be asking for twice the capital they think they need to reach stated milestones.

Investors like to hedge their bets. Any sales or market acceptance you can garner early on will enhance your case for funding down the road when scale-up needs arise. Having that practical, customer-centric knowledge and experience reflected in your plan should greatly increase your chances for success.

The business plan is seldom read cover to cover by investors, but it does serve as your proxy when you're not there. It informs investors on details concerning intellectual property, financial projections, and management team backgrounds. Although shows like *Shark Tank* are fun and interesting, they are not realistic from an investor trigger-pulling perspective. In reality, investors want to mull over all the information as a critical step in the due diligence process. Incidentally, it's worth noting that the *Shark Tank* investors are, paradoxically, relatively risk averse. They usually decline to invest when they find out that the presenting entrepreneurs have little or no sales traction. The sharks generally provide capital for expansion—not for riskier concept testing or market acceptance. They know from experience that events do not often unfold according to plan.

Another byproduct of the planning process should be rock solid presentations of varying lengths, including 30 seconds, 3 minutes, and 15 minutes. The first two are often called elevator and subway pitches, respectively. Entrepreneurs should be prepared to pitch the new venture almost anywhere. There is no substitute for a well-rehearsed, in-person, passionate solicitation of an entrepreneur's opportunity. The various permutations of the pitch are more important than the bound form of the business plan. Pitches should be done enthusiastically, but realistically. If you are not enthusiastic about your venture, how do you expect investors to feel?

I'll close this chapter old school-style with former D-Day commander and President of the United States, Dwight D. Eisenhower, who said, "In preparing for battle I have always found that plans are useless, but planning is indispensable."

Contra Maxims for Business Planning

A business plan is not absolutely necessary for entrepreneurial success. Combine business plan writing with tangible field or bench work. A business plan is not just for communicating value, it helps uncover value.

The work that goes into writing the business plan is more valuable than the final document. Lastly, make sure you have one heck of a convincing pitch!

Notes

1. Julian Lange, Aleksandar Mollov, Michael Pearlmutter, Sunil Singh and William Bygrave, "Pre-Start-up Formal Business Plans and Post-Start-up Performance: A Study of 116 New Ventures," *Venture Capital* 9, no. 4 (2007): 237–256.

2. *MIT Technology Review*, "Search Us, Says Google," 1 Nov 2000, https://www.technologyreview.com/s/400833/search-us-says-google/ (accessed Sep 29, 2016).

3. David Gumpert, *Burn Your Business Plan: What Investors Really Want from Entrepreneurs* (Needham, MA: Lauson Publishing Company, 2002).

4. Ibid.

5. Ibid.

6. David Kirsch, Brent Goldfarb and Azi Gera, "Form or Substance: The Role of Business Plans in Venture Capital Decision Making," *Strategic Management Journal* 30, (2009): 487–515.

7. Rafael Fernandez-Guerrero, Lorenzo Revuelto-Taboada and Virginia Simon-Moya, "The Business Plan as a Project: An Evaluation of its Predictive Capability for Business Success," *The Service Industries Journal* 32, no. 15 (2012): 2399–2420.

8. Tomas Karlsson and Benson Honig, "Judging a Business by its Cover: An Institutional Perspective on New Ventures and the Business Plan," *Journal of Business Venturing* 24, no. 1 (2009): 27–45.

9. Lange et al., "Pre-Start-up Formal Business Plans"

10. Ibid.

11. Simon Bridge and Cecil Hegarty, "An Alternative to Business Plan Advice for Start-ups?" *Industry and Higher Education* 26, no. 6 (2012): 443–452.

12. Maali Ashamalla, John Orife and Ivan Abel, "Business Plans: Are they Relevant to Venture Capitalists?" *Journal of Small Business and Entrepreneurship* 21, no. 4 (2008): 381–392.

13. Frederic Delmar and Scott Shane, "Does Business Planning Facilitate the Development of New Ventures?" *Strategic Management Journal* 24, no. 12 (2003): 1165–1185.

14. C.S. Chan and Haemin Park, "How Images and Color in Business Plans Influence Venture Investment Screening Decisions," *Journal of Business Venturing* 30, no. 5 (2015): 732–748.

15. Chana Schoenberger, "Avoid this Color in Your Business Plan," *The Wall Street Journal* 24, (Aug 2015): R4.

16. Jeffrey Timmons and Stephen Spinelli, *New Venture Creation: Entrepreneurship for the 21st Century, 7th ed.* (New York, NY: McGraw-Hill, 2007).

17. John Bean, *Engaging Ideas: The Professor's Guide to Integrating Writing, Critical Thinking, and Active Lessons in the Classroom* (San Francisco, CA: Jossey-Bass, 2001), 3.

18. Peter Thiel, *Zero to One: Notes on Start-ups, or How to Build the Future* (New York, NY: Crown Business, 2014), 2.

19. Ibid., 21

20. Dir. Daniel Geller & Dayna Goldfine, *Something Ventured* (Miralan Productions, DVD, 2011).

21. Daniel Kahneman, *Thinking, Fast and Slow* (New York: Farrar, Straus and Giroux, 2011), 250, 255.

Index

OTHER TITLES IN THE HUMAN RESOURCE MANAGEMENT AND ORGANIZATIONAL BEHAVIOR COLLECTION

- *The Illusion of Inclusion: Global Inclusion, Unconscious Bias, and the Bottom Line* by Helen Turnbull
- *On All Cylinders: The Entrepreneur's Handbook* by Ron Robinson
- *The Resilience Advantage: Stop Managing Stress and Find Your Resilience* by Richard S. Citrin and Alan Weiss
- *Successful Interviewing: A Talent-Focused Approach to Successful Recruitment and Selection* by Tony Miller
- *HR Analytics and Innovations in Workforce Planning* by Tony Miller
- *Success: Theory and Practice* by Michael Edmondson
- *Leading The Positive Organization: Actions, Tools, and Processes* by Thomas N. Duening, Donald G. Gardner, Dustin Bluhm, Andrew J. Czaplewski, and Thomas Martin Key
- *Performance Leadership* by Karen Moustafa Leonard and Fatma Pakdil
- *The New Leader: Harnessing The Power of Creativity to Produce Change* by Renee Kosiarek
- *Employee LEAPS: Leveraging Engagement by Applying Positive Strategies* by Kevin E. Phillips
- *Feet to the Fire: How to Exemplify and Create the Accountability That Creates Great Companies* by Lorraine A. Moore

Announcing the Business Expert Press Digital Library

Concise e-books business students need for classroom and research

This book can also be purchased in an e-book collection by your library as

- *a one-time purchase,*
- *that is owned forever,*
- *allows for simultaneous readers,*
- *has no restrictions on printing, and*
- *can be downloaded as PDFs from within the library community.*

Our digital library collections are a great solution to beat the rising cost of textbooks. E-books can be loaded into their course management systems or onto students' e-book readers. The **Business Expert Press** digital libraries are very affordable, with no obligation to buy in future years. For more information, please visit **www.businessexpertpress.com/librarians**. To set up a trial in the United States, please email **sales@businessexpertpress.com**.

www.ingramcontent.com/pod-product-compliance
Lightning Source LLC
Chambersburg PA
CBHW062023200326
41519CB00017B/4906